More Steamboat Simmers

by candy coleman

A Recipe Collection From The Friends Of
Routt Memorial Hospital Auxiliary

ISBN #0-943768-07-1

© Candy Coleman 1983

Published by Routt Memorial Hospital Auxiliary

Printed by Kwik-Kopy #25
1309 Main - Dallas, TX 75202

Cookbook Committee

ANNE SEVERSON, CHAIRMAN
JOYCE TAYLOR   JAN VAIL   PAT MADDOX

ARTIST - LIBBY RUSSELL

ACKNOWLEDGEMENTS

"The Historical Guide To Routt County"
   —The Tread Of Pioneers Museum

"Three Wire Winter"
   —Steamboat Springs High School

"Ski Town U.S.A."
   —John Rolfe Burroughs

"Steamboat Springs And The Treacherous & Speedy Skee"
   —Jean Wren

ROUTT MEMORIAL HOSPITAL

The Steamboat Springs Hospital Association was incorporated in December 1946 for the purpose of building a 25-bed hospital. Cash and pledges for the building totaled more than $100,000. With the aid of a ten-year mortgate the building was completed in 1950.

In one way or another, everyone in the community had a part in building the hospital. Dances, bazaars, and bake sales were held; cash donations and pledges were solicited, untold hours of work were volunteered by community organizations, and finally on August 13, 1950, the Routt County Memorial Hospital was dedicated to the people who made it happen.

Operating a hospital in the lean years of the early 50's was a constant struggle. Rates were raised from $8 double and $10 single to $10 and $12, but financial problems still plagued the small hospital. By 1954 it was apparent that the hospital needed additional help. The women of the community formed the Routt Memorial Hospital Auxiliary to fill that need.

The Auxiliary's committees secured donations of food and money. The women of the Auxiliary operated a thrift shop and donated many hours of service in the office, library, and as nurses' aids. They cleaned and mended, wheeled patients, made beds, and did what was needed of them to keep the hospital open.

2

In June of 1983 I met with the officers of the Auxiliary to discuss the concept of compiling a community cookbook as a fund-raising project. I had previously written "Steamboat Simmers" which had been well received but was no longer in print. The committee decided to proceed with the book; the title of "More Steamboat Simmers" was agreed upon. The cookbook was to incorporate the history of Steamboat Springs as well as other communities in Routt County, making it a book to read as well as to cook from. Profits from the sale of "More Steamboat Simmers" will be returned to the Routt Memorial Hospital Volunteer Auxiliary.

Platus said, "Where love has entered as the seasoning of food, I believe it will please anyone." I sincerely hope there was as much pleasing as love in "Steamboat Simmers," my first cookbook. None of the nine which followed has given me the sudden burst of joy I experienced when I first saw it in print. Alas, it is too dated to repeat. It gives me great pleasure to compile a new book patterned after that first labor of love about a town and its people. To know it will aid the community indeed creates "love as the seasoning of food."

I bring you thoughts of feasts,
hostess hints and menu treats...
Picnic baskets for the green of spring
and hot spiced wine for winter snow.
I bring you history of people and places to know,
and trails to hike as fall fills the skies with
aspen leaves of flaming gold and a spirit of
Thanksgiving.

I bring you...MORE STEAMBOAT SIMMERS...

Candy Coleman

Recipes from my personal collection are identified by the chef's hat.

"Steamboat Springs, Colorado, known far and wide as "Ski Town U.S.A." is more than a place on the map. It is a state of mind -- a shrine toward which the thoughts of the best skiers in the land, expatriate Steamboat-ites or not, turn longingly when the days begin to shorten and the snow begins to fall; a shrine to which they eagerly return year after year." -- John Rolfe Burroughs "Ski Town U.S.A." published by the Steamboat Springs Winter Sports Club, Inc.

The magical town of Steamboat Springs is nestled at a bend in the Yampa River and has been known by many names other than Ski Town U.S.A. Trappers called it "Big Bend" and, because of its many springs, often referred to it as "Bubbling Springs." The Ute Indians were convinced that the waters had miraculous healing powers and came from miles around to summer in the area; they called it "Medicine Springs."

Legend gives credit to three French trappers for finally giving the town a proper name. Located on the south bank of the Yampa River just east of the depot is a spring which at one time spouted water several feet into the air, making a loud chugging sound reminiscent of the sound of paddles on steamboats. On hearing this strange noise one of the trappers declared, "There's a steamboat, by gar!" By the 1870's everyone referred to the settlement as Steamboat Springs.

Since the first permanent settler arrived in 1873, the town of Steamboat Springs has seen many changes. By 1912, it had become the county seat and the recognized center of transportation and trade. When Norwegian Carl Howelsen arrived a year later with a pair of wooden skis slung over his shoulder and his pockets full of medals won in Scandinavian competitions, "Ski Town U.S.A." was born...he launched the recreation industry which has so greatly influenced the area's economy and life style.

Socrates is credited with writing, "So far as drinking is concerned, you have my hearty approval; for wine does of a truth moisten the soul and lull our griefs to sleep."

So, let's drink to the town of Steamboat Springs, Colorado... Ski Town U.S.A.

4

BUBBLING SPRINGS BUBBLY

A bubbly cooler for a summer day.

1 10-oz. pkg. frozen peaches in syrup, thawed	1 4/5-quart chilled pink champagne
1 Tbs. superfine sugar	Mint sprigs
Dash of cinnamon	

Place peaches, sugar, and cinnamon in blender container; cover. Puree until very smooth. Pour in champagne and blend for about 10 seconds. Pour over ice cubes and garnish with mint sprigs. Serves 6.

STEAMBOAT SIPPER: Combine 3 scoops of Coffee Ice Cream, 1 jigger brandy, 1/2 jigger creme de cacao in blender. Blend just until smooth. Serves 2.

--Anne Severson

"Then fill a fair and honest cup and bear it straight to me; The goblet hallows all it holds whate'er the liquid be."

--Oliver Wendell Holmes

CHILL CHASER

4 egg yolks	1¼ cups orange flavored liqueur
¼ cup honey, warmed	Grated orange rind
4 cups milk, scalded	Cinnamon sticks

Beat the egg yolks until thick and light; add the honey, in a stream, beating constantly. Beat in the scalded milk and liqueur. Serve in heated mugs and garnish with orange rind and a cinnamon stick. Serves 6.

As you lift your glasses high...serve something to nibble on...

CRAB DIP

2 Tbs. horseradish
8 ozs. cream cheese, softened
1 Tbs. milk
¼ tsp. salt

2 Tbs. minced onion
6½ ozs. crab meat (canned,
  fresh or frozen)
Slivered almonds, toasted

Combine the first six ingredients and spoon into a small dish (one you can serve from). Top with slivered almonds and bake at 350 degrees for 15 minutes or until heated through.

--*Kitty Ellison*

ZUCCHINI FINGERS

3 cups thinly sliced unpared
  zucchini
1 cup biscuit mix
½ cup onion, finely chopped
½ cup Parmesan cheese, grated
2 Tbs. parsley, chopped
½ tsp. salt

¼ tsp. seasoned salt
½ tsp. dried marjoram
Dash of pepper
Garlic powder to taste
½ cup salad oil
4 eggs, beaten

Grease a 13 x 9 x 2-inch pan. Mix all ingredients thoroughly. Pour into pan and bake until brown, about 25 minutes, at 350 degrees. Cut into 2 x 1-inch fingers and serve warm. Makes 4 dozen.

--*Maxine Elliott*

MUSHROOM TARTLETTES

24 slices fresh, thin-sliced
  white bread

2 Tbs. very soft butter

Filling:
4 Tbs. butter
3 Tbs. finely chopped shallots
½ lb. mushrooms, finely
  chopped
2 level Tbs. flour
1 cup heavy cream
½ tsp. salt

1/8 tsp. cayenne
1 Tbs. finely chopped parsley
1½ Tbs. finely chopped chives
½ tsp. lemon juice
2 Tbs. Parmesan cheese, grated
Butter

Coat the inside of 24 muffin tins heavily with butter. Cut a 3-inch round from each slice of bread and fit carefully into buttered tins (push the center of the bread into the well and gently press it around the bottom with the tips of your fingers).

Preheat oven to 400 degrees and bake the tartlettes for about 10 minutes or until lightly browned. Remove from tins and cool.

Saute shallots and mushrooms in butter. Add flour, stir in cream, salt, cayenne, parsley, chives and lemon juice. Stir until slightly thickened. Use a small spoon to fill the tartlettes and mound the filling slightly. Sprinkle each with Parmesan cheese. Dot with a tiny speck of butter and arrange tartlettes on a cookie sheet. Bake at 350 degrees for 10 minutes. Just before serving, run under the broiler, but watch them carefully as they burn easily.

NOTE: Unfilled tartlettes freeze well.

--*Birthe Wiik*
Scandinavian Lodge

WHISKEY DOGS

1 cup brown sugar
1 cup catsup

1 cup bourbon whiskey
1 16-oz. pkg. chicken or beef frankfurters

Cut frankfurters into bite size pieces and marinate several hours in the liquids. Heat over a low flame for 20 minutes; serve in a chafing dish.

WILD AND WONDERFUL WEINERS

2 pkgs. cocktail weiners
1 8-oz. jar red currant jelly
1 6-oz. jar yellow mustard

1 large onion, thinly sliced
2 Tbs. soy sauce

Cut the ends from the weiners and place in a baking dish. Combine the remaining ingredients and pour over the weiners. Bake for 3 hours at 250 degrees. Stir occasionally. Serve in a chafing dish with toothpicks.

"The soberest head doth once a day stand needful of a guide." — *Thurberville*

Carl Howelsen was born and raised in Norway. In 1913 at the age of 28 he came to Steamboat Springs and settled on a small ranch in Strawberry Park. Carl built a high platform on a steep slope and with the first snow began to pack it above and below. To everyone's surprise he tied skis onto his feet, climbed as far up the hill as possible, flew down the packed trail and hurtled through the air for at least 70 feet. He was immediately dubbed "that wild Swede out in the Park."

Howelsen brought the love of skiing and jumping to his new town. In 1914 he organized the first "Ski Carnival" and the following year built the ski jump on a steep hill south of town. It still bears his name, Howelsen Hill.

The wild Swede taught the area residents to bind their skis to their feet so that if they fell their skis wouldn't go sailing on down the mountain. He introduced grooved skis and a new pole easier to use.

Howelsen Hill

Howelsen also organized Sunday outings of cross-country skiing for pleasure. Fifty or more people took part in the all-day affairs. They packed lunches, carried a coffee pot large enough to accommodate everyone, and climbed uphill as far as six miles before gliding peacefully back home in the late afternoon. In those days the group was known as the "Ski Club"...it was the forerunner of today's Steamboat Winter Sports Club.

In these days of station wagons and paved roads it isn't necessary to hike great distances to a cross country ski area. Packing a picnic lunch for a winter outing is easy and fun. Take the soup in a thermos with throw-away hot cups in which to serve it. AND, don't forget the coffee pot!

COLD HAM MOUSSE

4 cups cooked ham, ground
1 large onion, diced
½ cup golden raisins
2-3 Tbs. dry sherry or madeira
1 tsp. prepared horseradish
½ tsp. ground nutmeg
2 tsp. Dijon mustard

2 Tbs. unflavored gelatin
2 Tbs. cold water
1 cup chicken stock
1 cup heavy cream
2 Tbs. finely chopped fresh parsley

Put the ground ham, onion, and raisins through the finest blade of a meat grinder 3 times. Place the meat mixture in a large bowl and add the sherry or madeira, horseradish, nutmeg, and mustard. Bring the chicken stock to a boil. Soften the gelatin in the water and dissolve the gelatin mixture in the boiling stock. Beat the dissolved gelatin into the ham mixture. Cool at room temperature approximately 10-15 minutes.

In a small bowl whip the cream until stiff and fold it into the ham mixture along with the parsley. Turn the mixture into an oiled 5-cup mold. Chill until set, approximately 3 hours. Serve with very thin slices of French bread or rye bread. The mousse would be nice on a picnic with cheese, wine, and Basque Pickled Beans. Serves 8-10.

MINESTRONE SOUP

¼ lb. salt pork
1 clove garlic, minced
1 onion, minced
1 tsp. basil
1 tsp. oregano
1 zucchini, sliced
1 carrot, sliced

1 tomato, peeled and chopped
3 or 4 spinach leaves, chopped
1 stalk celery, sliced
1 quart chicken broth
2 16-oz. cans white Great
  Northern Beans with juice
1 cup spaghetti, broken

Finely chop the salt pork. Brown in a large soup pot with the garlic, onion, and seasonings. Add the zucchini, carrot, tomato, spinach, celery and chicken broth. Simmer until vegetables are tender, but crisp. Add the beans and spaghetti. Simmer until the spaghetti is cooked. Serve with freshly grated Parmesan cheese sprinkled over each portion. Serves 6 to 8.

--Anne Severson

CHEESE BREAD

"A bread to serve with soups and stews!"

1 cup milk
3 Tbs. sugar
1 Tbs. salt
1 Tbs. butter

2 pkgs. yeast
1 cup water, warmed
4½ cups sifted flour
1 cup cheese, grated

Scald the milk and add the sugar, salt and butter. Cool. Dissolve the yeast in warm water and add the milk mixture. Add the flour and cheese and blend well. Cover and set in a warm place to double in bulk (about 45 minutes). Stir down and beat for 30 seconds. Turn into 2 small loaf pans, 1 large loaf pan, or a 1½-quart casserole, well greased. Bake at 350 degrees for 1 hour.

--Jayne Hill

ROASTED CHICKEN

This is excellent hot or cold.

1 large roasting chicken
Poultry seasoning
1 large onion

¼ cup butter
Vegetable oil
Seasoning salt

Dust the inside of chicken with poultry seasoning. Cut the
onion in quarters and place it and the butter inside. Rub the
outside with oil and sprinkle liberally with seasoning salt.
Bake, breast side down, for 30 minutes. Turn chicken and bake
an additional 30 minutes at 450 degrees. Serves 4 to 6.

--*Mindy Williams*

APPLESAUCE SPICE COOKIES

1 cup butter	1 tsp. nutmeg and cloves
2 eggs	2 tsps. cinnamon
2 cups brown sugar	2 cups raisins
2 cups applesauce	2 cups chopped nuts
2 tsps. soda	4 cups flour

Combine all the ingredients. Drop from teaspoon onto lightly
greased baking sheet. Bake at 350 degrees for about 12 minutes.

--*Jan Vail*

GARDEN VEGETABLE DIP

"This is a zesty, delicous dip!"

1 small green pepper	1 pint salad dressing
1 medium onion	1 tsp. lemon juice
Several sprigs fresh parsley	1 tsp. Worcestershire sauce

Place all ingredients in blender and blend until smooth.
Refrigerate at least 24 hours before serving. Serve with
an assortment of fresh vegetables for dipping.

--*Christine McKelvie*

PEANUT BUTTER CRISPS

3 cups quick cooking oats	½ tsp. salt
3/4 cup firmly packed brown sugar	½ cup butter or margarine
	1 cup chunky peanut butter

Combine oats, sugar and salt; set aside. Melt margarine and
add to oat mixture and mix well. Firmly pack half of mixture
into a 11 x 7-inch baking pan. Melt peanut butter and spread
evenly over oats. Cover with remaining oat mixture, packing
gently. Bake at 350 degrees 25 to 30 minutes. Let cool before cutting. Makes 18 squares.

The Yampa River derived its name from a pungent little tuber, yampa, which grows profusely along the river bottom...at least that's according to some historians. Yet confusion has always surrounded the source of the name "Yampa." Mountain men called the river the Bear River and thought yampa was an Indian word for bear. Others referred to yampa as a wild onion and further research revealed that oldtimers said the "pungent little tuber" belonged to the carrot family. To confuse you even more---the tubers resemble small sweet potatoes. Nonetheless, it is grown only in northwestern Colorado and is one of the best wild food plants of the area.

The proper name for this beautiful river winding its way through the valley is really of no consequence...it has become a favorite playground for the adventuresome. Kyak races are held over a tough course and on bright summer days you will find young and old alike floating merrily down the river on innertubes. Trout season lures the anglers to its banks.

You might plan a picnic on the banks of the Yampa River with the menu including an onion tart, a carrot salad or relish, and a sweet potato pie. At least one name will be right! But a word of caution...if you plan to harvest your ingredients from the Yampa River be certain you have the right plant---some in this pungent little tuber family are poisonous!

YAMPA ONION PIE

Pastry:
1½ cups flour
3/4 tsp. salt

1½ tsp. caraway seeds
½ cup shortening
2 to 3 Tbs. cold water

Combine flour, salt, and caraway seeds. Add shortening; cut into flour until mixture resembles coarse corn meal. Stir in water until mixture adheres and follows fork around bowl (or make in your food processor). Turn onto a floured board and roll to 1/8-inch thickness and fit into a 10-inch pie plate. Bake at 425 degrees for 10 minutes.

Filling:
6 slices bacon, cooked crisp and crumbled
3 cups thinly sliced onions
3 Tbs. butter, melted
½ cup milk

1½ cups sour cream
1 tsp. salt
2 eggs, well beaten
3 Tbs. flour

Cook onions in bacon fat until golden in color; drain fat and spoon onions into pie shell.
Add milk, 1¼ cups sour cream and salt to eggs. Blend flour with remaining ¼-cup sour cream and combine with egg mixture. Bake at 325 degrees for 30 minutes or until firm in center. Garnish with additional crisp bacon slices when serving as a main dish. Serves 8.

--Mrs. John Coleman
Germany

CARROT SALAD

3 cups grated carrots
1 tart apple, unpeeled, chopped
½ cup raisins
¼ cup toasted slivered almonds

1 cup sour cream
¼ cup mayonnaise
1 Tbs. lemon juice
¼ tsp. salt

Combine carrots, apples, raisins, and almonds in salad bowl. Blend together remaining ingredients and stir into salad. Serves 6.

SWEET POTATO PIE

1 cup sugar
2 tsps. cornstarch
½ tsp. salt
¼ tsp. each, cinnamon and nutmeg
Dash of cloves
3/4 cup dark corn syrup

3 Tbs. butter
1¼ cups cooked sweet potatoes, mashed
3 eggs lightly beaten
2 Tbs. bourbon
Unbaked 9-inch pie shell
¼ cup pecans, chopped

Combine sugar, cornstarch, salt, and spices in a saucepan; stir in corn syrup, butter and sweet potatoes. Bring to a boil over medium heat and boil, stirring, for 3 minutes or until thickened. Remove from heat and gradually stir in the beaten eggs. Add the bourbon. Pour into the pie shell and sprinkle top with pecans. Bake at 400 degrees for 10 minutes; reduce heat to 350 degrees and bake for 35 to 40 minutes, or until set. Makes 1 pie.

CARROT AND APRICOT RELISH

½ cup vinegar
2 Tbs. honey
¼ tsp. salt
1 cinnamon stick

1-1/3 cups shredded radishes
½ cup shredded carrots
8 dried apricots, cut in
   strips

Combine vinegar, honey, salt and cinnamon stick and boil for 3 minutes. Pour over remaining ingredients; cover and let marinate in refrigerator at least 30 minutes. Yummy with grilled pork or chicken. Makes 1 pint.

Not for picnics but an inexpensive main dish using sweet potatoes and leftover ham.

STUFFED SWEET POTATOES

3 large sweet potatoes
½ tsp. salt
2 Tbs. brown sugar
1 Tbs. prepared mustard
2 Tbs. butter

1/3 cup cream
1 cup diced ham
12 large marshmallows
Nutmeg

Bake potatoes in a 350 degree oven until done. Cut in half lengthwise and scoop out pulp; mash thoroughly. Add salt, sugar and mustard. Heat butter with milk until butter melts and combine it with the potatoes. Beat until fluffy. Fold in ham and pile into potato shells. Top each half with 2 marshmallows and sprinkle with nutmeg. Bake at 350 degrees for 20 minutes or until heated through. Serves 6.

--Malvina Carothers
Terrell, Texas

"When the moon is at the full
mushrooms you may freely pull;
But when the moon is on the wane
wait ere you think to pluck again."

This old English folk rhyme could easily apply to mushrooms
which also grow wild in the area. Unless you know your mushrooms, pick them from the grocer's shelf!

MUSHROOM CASSEROLE

6 slices white bread, buttered,
  cut into 1-inch squares
1 lb. fresh mushrooms,
  coarsely sliced
3 Tbs. butter
½ cup each, onion, celery,
  green pepper and pimiento,
  chopped
½ cup mayonnaise
3/4 tsp. salt
¼ tsp. pepper
2 eggs
1½ cups milk
1 can cream of mushroom soup,
  undiluted
2 slices bread, crusts removed
Cheddar cheese

Butter a casserole dish and place half of the bread squares in
bottom of dish. Saute the mushrooms in butter for several
minutes and combine with the chopped vegetables and mayonnaise.
Spread on top of bread squares and top with remaining bread
pieces. Beat eggs slightly with milk and pour over ingredients in casserole dish. Refrigerate 2 to 24 hours. When
ready to bake, spoon mushroom soup over all and top with 2
slices bread, diced. Bake at 325 degrees for 50 minutes; top
with grated Cheddar cheese and bake an additional 10 to 15
minutes. Serves 8.

--Lucille Butler

BAKED PEACHES: Top a can of drained peach halves with brown
sugar and sour cream. Bake 10 minutes at
350 degrees.

Steamboat At The Mountain

During the early years Howelsen Hill was the popular ski and jumping area in the town of Steamboat Springs. In 1955 Jim Temple, son of an early ranching family, spearheaded the creation of a new area at the base of Storm Mountain, two miles east of the town. On January 2, 1962, the exciting new hill opened with a 4,000 foot double chair lift, a poma lift, and a single A-frame building. The Thunderhead lift came in 1964 and Four Points was added in 1968. The bustling new ski mountain was renamed Mt. Werner in 1964 in honor of "Buddy" Werner who was born in Steamboat Springs and led America's challenge to skiers of Europe in the 50's and 60's. Tragically, in April 1964, he was killed in an avalanche in Switzerland while filming a ski movie.

The LTV Corporation of Dallas, Texas bought the ski area in 1969, and the building boom began. They built the Steamboat Village Inn, an eight-story hotel, a shopping plaza, and a Swiss engineered gondola, all to exacting standards of excellence...and they renamed the ski area Steamboat. By 1978 the Steamboat Ski Area had 13 chair lifts, two poma lifts, downhill trails up to 2-1/2 miles in length, and magnificent cross country trails. Tennis courts, an athletic club, riding stables and a spectacular 18-hole golf course had also been constructed to appeal to summer visitors. The original Steamboat Village Inn achieved overnight success. It was subsequently acquired by the Sheraton organization and renamed the Sheraton at Steamboat.

On May 1, 1979, the ski area was purchased by the Northwest Colorado Ski Corporation.

Whenever a corporation moves into a town it means new beginnings for families. Often flatlanders find themselves in the mountains, tropical residents must shop for snow attire, and new friends must be made. Extending a "welcome" hand by entertaining with a brunch to introduce your neighbor can make her new beginning one to remember...

BRUNCH EGGS

6 Tbs. butter
6 Tbs. flour
2 cups milk
1½ cups Cheese Whiz
1 cup sour cream

½ lb. fresh mushrooms
18 to 20 hard-cooked eggs
1 lb. bacon, crisp cooked and
  crumbled

Melt butter and add flour; stir until blended. Slowly add the milk and cook until sauce is thick, stirring constantly. Add the Cheese Whiz and sour cream and blend. Set aside to cool. Slice mushrooms and saute in butter for 3 minutes. Slice the hard-cooked eggs. Layer cream sauce, mushrooms, eggs and bacon in a large casserole; repeat layers ending with bacon. Bake at 350 degrees until hot and bubbly. Can be made ahead. Serves 12 to 14.

--Ruth McGuyrt

GLAZED SAUSAGES

3 Tbs. butter
2 large unpeeled apples,
  sliced
1 tsp. cinnamon
¼ tsp. each, cloves and nutmeg
1 Tbs. cornstarch
1 cup cranberry-apple juice

1 lb. Italian sausage, cooked,
  cut in 3/4-inch slices
3/4 lb. kielbasa, cooked, cut
  in 3/4-inch slices
1 pkg. brown and serve sausage
  links, cooked

Melt butter and saute apple slices. Sprinkle with cinnamon, cloves and nutmeg as they cook over medium heat until barely tender, stirring occasionally. Remove but reserve juices in pan. Blend in cornstarch and add the cranberry-apple juice. Stir until mixture thickens. Arrange cooked meats and apples in a chafing dish and pour cranberry glaze over all. Cook until heated through. Keep hot in a chafing dish. Serves 8.

--Ruth McGuyrt

HOT WHITE WINE: Two cups Rhine wine, 3 Tbs. Galliano, 3 Tbs. honey, 1 Tbs. sugar and 4 tsp. butter. Bring to a boil and pour into heated mugs. Garnish with orange slices and a cinnamon stick. Serves 4.

GRITS STUFFED MUSHROOMS

12 large mushrooms
1 cup cooked grits
1/3 cup Parmesan cheese
1 Tbs. chopped parsley
½ tsp. dry mustard

½ tsp. thyme
½ tsp. salt
Pepper to taste
Black walnuts, chopped

Remove stems from mushrooms and save for use in soups, etc. Combine remaining ingredients, except nuts, and fill mushrooms. Top with chopped black walnuts (or sunflower seeds) and bake at 350 degrees for 15 minutes.

FRUIT COMPOTE

1 box mixed dried fruit
1 cup water
1½ tsps. horseradish
2 Tbs. vinegar

2 Tbs. brandy
3/4 tsp. cinnamon
Dash of nutmeg

Cook fruit about 20 minutes in the water; drain off half the liquid. Add the remaining ingredients and heat but do not boil. If fruit is not to desired doneness, cook, without boiling, a few minutes longer. Let stand several hours for flavors to mingle. Serve warm or chilled. Serves 6.

--Jean Schriber
Pennsylvania

APPLESAUCE BRAN MUFFINS

1¼ cups sifted flour
3 tsps. baking powder
½ tsp. salt
2 Tbs. sugar
1 cup bran

1 egg, beaten
1/3 cup milk
2/3 cup applesauce
¼ cup melted margarine

Sift the dry ingredients; mix in bran. Combine the remaining ingredients and add all at once, stirring only enough to moisten. Fill greased muffin pans 2/3 full. Bake at 400 degrees about 20 minutes. Makes 12.

--Lillian Hagan

CRANBERRY ORANGE RING

A rosy crown of cranberry-orange relish tops a biscuit ring.

½ cup cranberry-orange relish
1 Tbs. light corn syrup
4 Tbs. melted butter
½ cup brown sugar

1 tsp. cinnamon
2 pkgs. refrigerated biscuits
Finely chopped nuts (optional)

Combine cranberry relish and corn syrup; heat just to boiling (40 seconds in the microwave oven). Spoon mixture into a greased 6½-cup ring mold. Combine butter, sugar and cinnamon (add the nuts if desired) and spread one side of each biscuit with some of the mixture. Place biscuits on edge in ring mold. Bake at 375 degrees for 25 minutes. Allow to cool about 3 minutes; invert onto serving plate. Makes 20 rolls.

BLUEBERRY TOPPED CHEESE PIE

1 3-oz. pkg. cream cheese
½ cup powdered sugar
½ tsp. vanilla
1 cup whipping cream

1 Graham Cracker Crust
1 Tbs. lemon juice
1 1-lb. 5-oz. can blueberry
  pie filling

Cream together cheese, powdered sugar and vanilla. Whip cream until stiff, not dry, and fold it in. Turn into prepared pastry shell and spread evenly. Stir lemon juice into pie filling and carefully spoon over the cheese filling. Chill.

Crust:

1½ cups Graham Crackers,
  crushed

1/3 cup butter, melted
2 Tbs. sugar

Combine and press into a 9-inch pie plate. Bake at 350 degrees for 10 minutes. Cool.

--June Kinney

*"The discovery of a new dish confers
more happiness on humanity than the
discovery of a new star."*
—Brillat-Savarin

There were many Mt. Werner pioneers responsible for carving
out this winter wonderland. Gerald Groswold, William Sayre,
Sam Huddleston, John McCready, and Hank Perry struggled
with architecture, landscaping and financing to bring a dream
to fruition. John Fetcher (page 25), Harvard engineer turned
rancher, was the first company president. Marvin Crawford
and Gordy Wren, both Olympic skiers, were area managers. All
anxiously awaited opening day.

January 12, 1963 dawned bitter cold...40 degrees below zero!
There was an A-frame building, the Christie lift, a poma on
the beginners' hill and open country on all sides for as far
as the eye could see. The day was doomed from the very beginning. Only one lonely skier braved the elements for this
auspicious occasion and perhaps he wishes he hadn't. Hank
Perry had driven in from Denver managing the treacherous
passes and the Continental Divide without mishap only to
skid into the only car in the parking lot...the one belonging
to the lonely skier!

The day finally came to an end and is now laughingly remem-
bered. Within a few short years national interest helped
turn the new ski area into the popular resort it is today.
With champions like Gordy Wren and Marvin Crawford on the
team...it had to be a winner!

In 1948 Gordy Wren set two standing records. He was the
first American to qualify in all four Olympic ski events...
slalom, downhill, cross country and jumping...and he placed
fifth in jumping, the highest an American competitor has ever
achieved. He came to Steamboat as instructor of the ski
teams from 1949 to 1954. He coached Buddy, Loris, and Skeeter
Werner as well as Marvin Crawford. His wife, Jean, is an
author and columnist for the Steamboat Pilot and says this is
one of Gordy's favorites...

CHICKEN CACCIATORE

1 chicken, cut in pieces
¼ green pepper, diced
4 cloves garlic, thinly sliced
1 4½-oz. jar sliced mushrooms
½ small onion, diced
1 28-oz. can tomato sauce
Onion powder to taste,
  optional

1 28-oz. can tomatoes,
  broken up
1½ tsps. sweet basil
1½ tsps. parsley
3 bay leaves
Salt and garlic powder to
  taste

Brown chicken pieces in hot oil. Remove from pan and brown the green pepper, onion, garlic and mushrooms in remaining oil. Drain any collected liquids and oil. Add the tomato sauce, tomatoes, and spices; bring to a boil. Reduce heat to a simmer and cook for 1 hour. Add the chicken. Continue to cook for 45 minutes to 1 hour. Serve over cooked spaghetti. Serves 4 to 6.

--Jean Wren

From 1947 when Marvin Crawford placed first in the National Junior Jumping Championships, to 1956 when he became a member of the Nordic Combined Olympic Team in Cortina, Italy, he was a champion. And his sons have followed in his footsteps with Gary Crawford on the U.S. Olympic team in 1980 and a hopeful for '84. Edie Crawford has held her championship family together with a love of home and says all three of her boys have enjoyed this pie for their birthdays the past 20 years...

SWISS CHOCOLATE PIE

¼ lb. butter (1 stick)
3/4 cup sugar
2 squares baking chocolate

1 tsp. vanilla
2 eggs

Melt butter and chocolate in saucepan; add sugar and vanilla. Beat in eggs one at a time. Pour into a baked 9-inch pie shell. (If using a deep dish pie shell, make the recipe 1½ times.) Top with whipped cream.

--Edie Crawford

CRESCENT ZUCCHINI PIE

4 cups thinly sliced unpared
  zucchini
1 cup chopped onion
½ cup butter or margarine
½ cup chopped parsley OR
2 Tbs. dried parsley flakes
½ tsp. salt
½ tsp. pepper
¼ tsp. garlic powder

¼ tsp. sweet basil leaves
¼ tsp. oregano
2 eggs
8 ozs. Muenster or Mozzarella
  cheese
1 8-oz. pkg. Crescent dinner
  rolls
2 tsps. mustard

Saute zucchini and onion in butter about 10 minutes. Stir in
the parsley, salt, pepper, garlic powder, basil and oregano.
In a large bowl, beat the eggs and add the cheese; stir in
the vegetable mixture.
Press the dinner rolls over bottom and sides of a 10-inch
quiche pan. Spread the mustard over the crust; top with
vegetable mixture. Bake at 375 degrees for about 30 minutes.
Serves 4 to 6.

--Dottie Schnackenberg

MOM'S SWEET AND SOUR BEANS

Good made the day before serving.

3 slices bacon
1 medium onion, chopped
½ cup catsup
½ cup sugar

¼ cup vinegar
2 16-oz. can French style
  green beans, drained

Saute the bacon until crisp. Cook onion in bacon grease
until transparent. Drain off the grease. Crumble bacon and
return to pan; add catsup, vinegar and sugar and simmer
until mixture is thickened. Combine the sauce and green
beans in a casserole dish. Heat until hot and bubbly.
Serves 6.

--Betty Christoff

The Gondola

Mt. Werner   1.93

Wally Schirra and Alan Shepard, former astronauts, were frequent visitors during the early days of the Steamboat ski
area. Wally just happened to be in town the night before LTV
was to test run the shiny new gondola. He was having great
sport teasing company officials about their "countdown," so
it was suggested he take the ride. He gracefully declined
adding that he was afraid of heights!

*My! how things do change...now we have put a woman, Sally
Ride, into outer space. The average woman wouldn't want to
fly so high, but creating a souffle rising to fantastic
heights just might be your own countdown to fame...*

CRABMEAT SOUFFLE

Prepare one day in advance:

8 to 10 slices white bread,
  trimmed and cut in 1-inch
  cubes
2 cups crabmeat
½ cup mayonnaise
1 medium onion, chopped
1 green pepper, chopped

1 cup celery, chopped
Salt and pepper to taste
1 can cream of mushroom soup
2 cups milk
4 eggs, beaten
1½ cups grated Cheddar cheese

Spread half of the bread cubes in a baking dish. Mix crab-meat, mayonnaise, onion, green pepper, celery, salt, pepper and mushroom soup. Spread over bread cubes. Put remaining bread cubes on top. Blend milk and eggs and pour on top of casserole. Refrigerate overnight. Bring to room temperature; top with cheese and bake at 350 degrees for 1 hour. Serves 8.

--Anne Severson

BRUNCH EGGS ELEGANTE

2 cups grated sharp cheese
¼ cup butter
1 cup half and half
¼ tsp. salt

½ tsp. fresh cracked pepper
2 tsps. prepared mustard
12 eggs, slightly beaten

Spread cheese in a buttered 9 x 13-inch baking dish; dot with butter. Combine cream, salt, pepper and mustard. Pour half the mixture over cheese; carefully top with the beaten eggs. Pour remaining cream mixture over eggs. Bake at 325 degrees for 50 to 60 minutes or until set. Can be made the night before, covered with foil and refrigerated until baking time. Serves 8 to 10.

--Virginia Silk

Either of the above recipes would make a marvelous brunch or luncheon main dish. A "fruity" type of salad is a nice accompaniment for eggs.

CHERRY COKE SALAD

1 16-oz. can sour red cherries
1 16-oz. can crushed pineapple, chilled
1 cup pecans, chopped

2 3-oz. boxes cherry Jello
1 cup sugar
1 cup water
1 small bottle Coke, chilled

Cook cherries with juice, water and sugar. Boil 2 minutes. Pour over Jello and let set till syrupy. Add chilled pine-apply, juice, and nuts. Stir in the well chilled Coke. Pour into a 9 x 13-inch pan and chill until set. Cut in squares and serve on a chilled lettuce leaf. Serves 8 to 10.

--Beverly Callant

A DIFFERENT MARBLE CAKE

1 pkg. yellow cake mix
1 pkg. instant vanilla
  pudding mix

1 8-oz. carton sour cream
½ cup oil
4 eggs

Combine and beat about 7 minutes on medium mixer speed.

Topping:
½ cup sugar
2 Tbs. brown sugar

2 Tbs. cocoa
1 tsp. cinnamon

Combine and set aside.
Grease and flour a tube or Bundt pan. Pour half of batter
into prepared pan. Cover with half of topping mixture. Pour
in remaining batter and mix lightly. Cover with remaining
topping. Bake at 350 degrees for 1 hour or until pick inserted in center comes out clean.

--Mindy Williams

*It is lovingly said that John Fetcher literally carved out
some of the ski trails with his hands and carried the first
gondola on his shoulders to the top. He engaged the Swiss
firm that built the gondola and unlike our astronauts was
eager to hop aboard for the test ride. He is now in the Ski
Hall of Fame, a tribute to his ski area engineering accom-
plishments. His wife, Chris, says this is his favorite pie.*

JOHN'S RHUBARB PIE

1 9-inch double pie crust
1 egg white
4 cups rhubarb, diced

4 Tbs. flour
1¼ cups sugar
1 Tbs. butter

Brush the bottom pie crust with egg white. Combine rhubarb,
flour and sugar and arrange in pie dish. Dot with butter.
Either cut a hole in the center of the top crust to let steam
escape or make a lattice type top crust. Dot top crust with
an additional tablespoon butter. Bake at 400 degrees for
about 45 minutes, or until crust is nicely browned. Turn off
heat, but leave pie in oven and open the door. The fruit
continues to simmer, but the pastry does not continue to
brown. Let pie cool in the oven.

--Chris Fetcher

Winter Carnival

February 10, 1914 dawned warmer than usual but the excitement of Steamboat residents closely resembled a raging inferno... the first Winter Carnival was to begin at 9:00 a.m. and there were contests and games scheduled for everyone. Although nearly 2,000 had come to witness the events, little did they know it was to be the beginning of a tradition.

During those early years there were three major activities... ski jumping for the courageous, cross country racing for the not-so-courageous, and "street events" for everyone. The latter included races for the very young, skijoring, and skijoring hurdle races. They are still a part of the festivities which are held the second weekend of every February. Now you will find slalom and downhill races at Mt. Werner, a costumed parade, and a magnificent night show followed by the crowning, usually by the Governor of Colorado, of the Carnival Queen.

Governor and Mrs. Lamm entertain at the Governor's Mansion in Denver using fresh rainbow or mountain trout from Colorado streams and asparagus which grows wild on the Western Slope. The following recipes from Dorothy Lamm would create a marvelous menu to serve visitors to the Winter Carnival.

ASPARAGUS SALAD

(Asparagus grows wild on the Western Slope of Colorado)

2 10-oz. pkgs. frozen asparagus spears or equal amount of fresh asparagus
1 can water chestnuts, drained and sliced
1 large or 2 small tomatoes, coarsely chopped
1 medium size onion, thinly sliced, separated into rings

Cook asparagus according to package directions or boil fresh asparagus for 12 minutes. Drain and cut each spear into thirds. Place warm asparagus into bowl. Add salad dressing of your choice. Chill one hour. Add other ingredients. Toss and drain. Serves 6 - 8.

--Dorothy Lamm
Governor's Mansion

COLORADO MOUNTAIN TROUT OR RAINBOW TROUT

Fresh or thawed.

Poach trout filet in a small amount of champagne. Not more
than 5 minutes. Over a low heat. If you were poaching 4
medium size trout in a skillet, you would use approximately
½ cup champagne.

Remove fish, and save 4 Tbs. of juice from champagne and
fish juice. If not 4 Tbs. left, add more champagne.

Add 1 cup of cream, simmer slowly till about half of mixture
is left. Add 1 cup of shredded sorrel and ¼ cup green peppercorns.

Reduce (simmer down) to desired thickness. Pour sauce over
filets and serve.   --*Governor's Mansion, Denver, Colorado*

*If you don't happen to have trout in your freezer, build your
menu around Colorado lamb.*

LAMB IN CABBAGE

4 lbs. boneless lamb, cubed	3 Tbs. flour
2 medium green cabbages, sliced	1 Tbs. whole peppercorns
	Boiling water to cover
4 Tbs. butter	Salt to taste

Brown meat lightly in hot butter. In a large pot, arrange
meat and cabbage in alternate layers. Pour on boiling water
to cover. When it has returned to the boiling point, cover
and simmer *very* slowly until meat is thoroughly cooked,
about 2 hours. If necessary, add more water from time to
time, but remember that cabbage gives off liquid. Serves 8.

CURRIED GRAPES: Heat green seedless grapes in chicken broth;
season with curry powder and serve with a
small lemon wedge. Marvelous with chicken
or pork.

WILD RICE CASSEROLE

2 cups boiling water
2/3 cup uncooked wild rice
1 cup Chicken Rice Soup
1 small can mushrooms,
  undrained
½ cup beef or chicken broth
1 tsp. salt

1 bay leaf
¼ tsp. each celery salt,
  garlic salt, pepper,
  onion salt, paprika
3 Tbs. chopped onion
3 Tbs. vegetable oil

Pour boiling water over rice; let stand, covered, 15 minutes.
Drain and place in a 2-quart casserole. Add soup, mushrooms
and liquid, water and seasonings. Mix gently and let stand
5 minutes. Saute onion in oil until glossy. Remove and
add to the casserole. Bake, covered, at 325 degrees for 2
hours. Serves 6 to 8.

--Mrs. William A. Bowes

MARINATED CARROTS

2 lbs. carrots
½ medium onion, sliced
¼ bell pepper, chopped
1 can tomato soup

½ cup vinegar
¼ cup oil
½ cup sugar
Tabasco to taste

Slice carrots in thin rounds. Boil in salted water 10
minutes. Drain well. Add onion and peper and mix gently.
Bring soup, vinegar, oil and sugar to boil in saucepan.
Add Tabasco. Pour over carrots and cover in airtight container overnight. Heat when ready to serve.

--Susan Bryant

POT DE CREME

1 6-oz. pkg. chocolate chips
Dash of salt
1 Tbs. rum or vanilla extract

2 Tbs. sugar
1 egg
3/4 cup milk

Heat milk to boiling point (do not boil). Put the remaining
ingredients in a blender; add milk and blend for one minute
on low. Pour into six small glasses or cups and chill at
least two hours. Top with whipped cream and chocolate curls.
Serves 6.

--Cookbook Committee

Carnival Games

Skijoring, one of the most exciting street events of Winter Carnival, is similar to a rodeo on skis. The course is customarily a city block in length. Horseback rider and skier make a team and each team runs against time. The horse, towing a skier at the end of a thirty foot rope, is allowed to reach top speed before the starting line.

The skijoring ring race is an extension of skijoring. Brass ring are dangled from standards at the side of the course down Lincoln Avenue. Riders on horseback attempt to collect as many rings as possible on a lance; racers are penalized two seconds for each ring missed.

Over the years men and women have engaged in the sport of collecting gold rings...not on a lance but on the third finger, left hand. Wedding vows are said, rings exchanged, and the prize is a lifetime of happiness---hopefully. For weddings, teas, or afternoon nibbling any of the following deserves a gold ring...

CELEBRATION SANDWICH

3/4 cup Roquefort or blue
   cheese
1 cucumber
3 tsps. brandy

1 loaf thin sliced white bread
Butter, softened
Parsley

Combine cheese and brandy. Wash cucumber and score the skin lengthwise with fork tines to create a decorative edge.
Slice into thin rounds. Refrigerate, covered, at least 30 minutes.
Using a 2-inch cookie cutter, cut 20 rounds out of the bread slices. Spread with softened butter and top with a cucumber slice. Spoon ½-teaspoon of cheese mixture in center of slice. Garnish with a parsley cluster. Makes 20 open-faced sandwiches.

WATERCRESS ROUNDS

6 hard-cooked eggs	1 tsp. salt
3 Tbs. mayonnaise	18 slices white bread
1 Tbs. Dijon mustard	1 bunch watercress, washed
2 tsps. grated onion	and chilled

Finely chop eggs and combine with mayonnaise, mustard, onion and salt. Mix until smooth. Cut 2½-inch rounds from bread and spread egg mixture on rounds. Garnish with watercress. Place on a cookie sheet; cover with plastic wrap and refrigerate until serving. Makes 36.

NOTE: The addition of 1 tsp. curry powder makes an entirely different taste treat.

ORANGE SANDWICHES ON MARMALADE NUT BREAD

¼ cup butter	1 Tbs. grated orange peel
½ cup confectioners' sugar, sifted	1½ tsps. lemon juice
	Dash of nutmeg

Combine all the ingredients and beat until light and fluffy. Spread on thin slices of Marmalade Nut Bread.

MARMALADE NUT BREAD

½ cup butter or margarine	1 tsp. salt
½ cup brown sugar, packed	½ tsp. baking soda
1 10-oz. jar orange marmalade	½ cup orange juice
2 eggs	½ cup chopped pecans or
2-3/4 cups flour	walnuts
2 tsps. baking powder	

Grease and flour bottom and sides of a 9 x 5 inch loaf pan. Cream butter and sugar until light and fluffy; add eggs, one at a time, mixing well after each addition. Blend in marmalade.
Combine the dry ingredients and add to the sugar mixture alternately with the orange juice. Mix well and stir in nuts. Spoon into prepared pan and bake at 325 degreed for 1 hour and 20 minutes or until pick inserted in center comes out clean. Cool 10 minutes and remove from pan to rack to cool. Spread with orange butter mixture and cut in fingers to serve. Makes 1 loaf.

RHUBARB DREAM BARS

2 cups flour   1 cup butter
3/4 cup confectioners' sugar

Combine flour and sugar; cut in butter until crumbs form.
Press onto bottom of a 15 x 10 x 1-inch jelly roll pan.
Bake at 350 degrees for 15 minutes. While crust is baking,
prepare filling.

Filling:

4 eggs   ½ tsp. salt
2 cups sugar   4 cups rhubarb, diced
½ cup flour

Blend eggs, sugar, flour and salt until smooth. Fold in
rhubarb.
Spread mixture over hot crust and return to oven. Bake for
40 to 45 minutes or until filling is lightly browned. Cool,
cut into squares or bars. Very good served warm with ice
cream or whipped cream.

--Shirley Zabel

MAKE BELIEVE FRENCH PASTRY

Line an 8 x 10-inch pan with a layer of whole Graham Crackers.
Make a package of coconut cream or vanilla instant pudding
mix to package directions and spread on top of crackers.
Add another layer of Graham Crackers.
Make a package of Dream Whip to package directions and spread
on top of crackers. Add another layer of Graham Crackers.
Make a thin frosting of powdered sugar, cream, and vanilla to
taste.
Frost the top layer of crackers.
Melt about 1 cup of chocolate chips and dribble over top in a
check pattern.
This should be refrigerated and is best made 24 hours in ad-
vance of serving. Serves 8.

--Cherrie Romanowski

The Lighted Man

Night falls on the carnival, but the fun is just beginning. Crowds flock to Howelsen Hill for the night show. The performers are local junior ski racers and ski patrolmen from the mountain. They carry lighted flares, jump through firey hoops, and ski in unison creating a serpentine line of brilliance down the hill...then comes the main attraction, Claudius Banks.

For more than forty years Banks has thrilled residents and visitors to the area. He attended Steamboat Winter Carnival in 1936 and decided the show needed his specialty...lights. He outlined his body and skis with lights, lugged the heavy and clumsy battery operated paraphernalia halfway up Howelsen Hill during the 1938 carnival and skied into history. To that first suit he added a helmet; a big spiral that soared six feet above his head ablaze with lights. Then he made the lights flash. He added signs. The last one read "Ski Town U.S.A." Banks didn't get to light all the letters because carnival was held during a blizzard! He has caught fire several times and had difficulty in convincing his sons, Jon and Kent, to join him in this show of shows. Jon has performed every year since 1971 alone or with his father and once all three thrilled the audience.

Each year a member, or members, of the Banks family lights a hillside and rekindles a lasting memory of Winter Carnival at Steamboat Springs...

Since visitors come from miles around to witness the light show and the two-day spectacle of Winter Carnival, it is party time in Steamboat. Brunches, cocktail parties, dinners and open houses honor the guests. Often late, late suppers following the night show are served before roaring fires in the comfort of family rooms throughout the community. The following menu can be prepared ahead of time and would warm any chilly evening...

BEEF STEW WITH WINE

1½ lbs. beef chuck, cut in
   1-inch cubes
1 Tbs. shortening
1 clove garlic
1 medium onion, chopped
½ tsp. salt
1/8 tsp. pepper
1 10-oz. can tomato soup

3/4 cup dry red wine
¼ cup water
¼ tsp. each, basil and thyme
½ cup catsup
3 carrots, sliced
1½ cups celery, diced
4 potatoes, diced

Brown the beef in shortening; add onion and garlic and saute
until onion is transparent. Add salt, pepper, soup, wine,
and water; cover and simmer 30 minutes. Add the remaining
ingredients and simmer for 1½ to 2 hours, covered. Recipe
can be doubled for a larger crowd, made ahead and reheated
when ready to serve. Serves 4.

--Jan Vail

*Serve the beef stew over (or with) this delectably short
puff pastry. It is also good cut in 1 x 3-inch fingers to
serve with salads.*

PUFF PASTRY

2 cups sifted flour
2½ tsps. baking powder
1 tsp. salt

1/3 cup corn meal
3/4 cup shortening
3/4 cup milk

Preheat oven to 450 degrees. Sift dry ingredients together
and cut in shortening with pastry blender. Add milk and
stir. On floured board, roll dough to ¼-inch thick. Cut in
rounds, squares, or fingers. Bake on ungreased cookie sheet
10 to 15 minutes. Makes 24 pieces.

FROZEN FRUIT SALAD

½ cup coarsely chopped nuts
¼ cup marachino cherries,
   chopped fine and drained
1 cup shredded coconut
3/4 cup drained crushed
   pineapple

2 cups sour cream
3/4 cup sugar
2 Tbs. lemon juice
1/8 tsp. salt
1 banana, diced

Blend together sour cream, sugar, lemon juice and salt. Fold in remaining ingredients. Spoon into paper lined muffin tins and freeze until firm. To serve, remove from freezer and allow to soften slightly. Remove muffin papers and serve on a salad lettuce leaf. Makes 12.

--Pat Maddox

SATIN PIE

1 9-inch baked pie shell
3/4 cup butter
1 cup sugar
3/4 cup cocoa
4 eggs

1 tsp. vanilla
½ tsp. almond extract
Nuts and whipped cream
   (optional)

Whip butter. Sift sugar and cocoa together and add to butter slowly on low mixer speed. If mixture becomes stiff; add 1 egg. Add remining eggs, one at a time, and beat on high until mixture is consistency of whipped cream. Add vanilla and almond extract; blend well and pour into baked pie shell. Refrigerate 2 hours. Sprinkle with nuts and serve topped with whipped cream if desired. Makes 1 pie.

--Marilyn McCaulley

HOT CHICKEN DIP

1 can cream of mushroom soup
1 8-oz. pkg. cream cheese
   with chives
1 5-oz. can chunk white
   chicken
¼ cup slivered almonds

2-oz. can sliced mushrooms,
   drained
½ tsp. Worcestershire sauce
Garlic powder and pepper
   to taste
2 tsps. sherry (optional)

Combine ingredients in a 1-quart fondue pot or saucepan. Cook over medium heat, stirring often, until hot. Serve with chips. Makes 3½ cups.

APPLE-ONION BAKE: Slice 6 tart apples and 5 large onions in thin slices. Alternate apples and onions in 4 layers in a buttered baking dish. Dot each layer with 1 tablespoon butter and sprinkle with 2 tablespoons brown sugar. Bake at 325 degrees for 2 hours or until apples are brown and casserole is about half full. Excellent holiday dish for turkey dinners. Serves 6.

 *The Ski Band*

It doesn't have seventy-six trombones, but the brain child of a public school music teacher, Franklin Evans, has skis. The school band toots their horns, beats their drums, marches in unison and doesn't miss a beat...all on skis. The Steamboat Springs Ski Band is the star of the Winter Carnival Parade and there is not another like it in the country.

To ski one normally needs snow but if you were a member of a ski marching band you would think it a necessity. No so. The ski band was invited to participate in the National Convention of Lion's Clubs in Chicago in the 50's. The month was July and everyone knows it doesn't snow in July, even for a ski band. What to do? Not wanting to miss the convention, they added wheels to their skis with an attachment to keep them from rolling backwards, and tootled their way to fame. Thoreau would possibly have said they were "marching to a different drummer."

The addition of pickles to this beef recipe makes it as different as wheels on skis...AND, it might make you famous!

DILL PICKLE ROLLS

1 lb. bacon	2 cans tomato soup
1 to 2 lbs. round steak	1 cup water
Dill pickle spears	1 onion, chopped

Cut round steak into strips 3 inches long by 1-inch wide. Roll steak strip around dill pickle spear. Roll a slice of bacon around each steak roll; fasten with toothpicks. Brown in a frying pan, turning often. Drain off fat. Combine tomato soup, water and onion; pour over the steak rolls. Cover and simmer for 2 to 3 hours. Serves 6.

--Michele Haller

 BUTTERSCOTCH SQUASH: Stir in some butterscotch pieces and chopped walnuts along with butter, salt, and pepper. Adds crunch and flavor.

*Serve the Dill Pickle Rolls with hot mashed potatoes or
noodles...or for another different taste treat try them with -*

PENNSYLVANIA DUTCH POTATO DUMPLINGS

3 cups cold mashed potatoes
3/4 to 1 cup flour
2 egg yolks
3/4 cup grated Parmesan or
   Swiss cheese

½ tsp. grated nutmeg
¼ cup butter, melted
1½ tsps. salt
½ tsp. pepper

Turn potatoes onto lightly floured board. Add flour, egg
yolks, ½ cup cheese and the nutmeg. Working with your hands,
combine ingredients until of kneading consistency, adding
more flour if necessary. Form into ropes, about 1-inch in
diameter; slice into 1-inch pieces. Press edges with tines
of fork.
Cook dumplings 10 at a time in a large pot of boiling salted
water. Cook about 10 minutes or until they float. Remove
and drain on paper toweling. Keep hot in a single layer in
an oven-proof dish in a warm oven. When ready to serve
(dumplings can be kept in oven up to 30 minutes), pour butter
over dumplings; sprinkle with salt, pepper and ¼ cup cheese.

NOTE: The sauce from the Dill Pickle Rolls is also good
       spooned over the dumplings.

TOM'S PECAN PIE

1 unbaked 9-inch pie shell
3 eggs
3/4 cup sugar
1 cup dark corn syrup

3/4 cup pecans, chopped
2 Tbs. melted butter
½ tsp. vanilla
Pinch of salt

Combine sugar, syrup, and eggs; mix well and add vanilla and
butter. Sprinkle pecans in pie shell and top with egg mixture. Bake at 225 degrees for 3½ to 4 hours. The baking
time is very important. Makes 1 pie.

--Judy Coleman (Mrs. Tom) Bowden

Many mothers having trouble managing Giggle Gulch and Head-wall find it thrilling to see tots of four and five years calmly skiing over a diminutive take-off to leap six or eight feet and skillfully turn at the end of the out run. This early learning at the hands of expert instructors is one of the reasons Steamboat produces so many fine skiers and jumpers.

The Steamboat Springs School District cooperates with the Winter Sports Club, pays an instructor, and offers two classes a week for pre-school-age children. The kids even have their very own organization known as the "Little Toot Ski Club." And now you know why all the children in Steamboat out-ski their parents!

For your own Little Toot after a day on the hill...

OATMEAL CRISPIES

Great to have on hand in the freezer for fresh cookies any time.

3/4 cup flour, sifted	1½ cups rolled oats, uncooked
½ tsp. salt	½ cup brown sugar
½ tsp. soda	½ cup granulated sugar
½ cup margarine or shortening	1 egg
	½ tsp. vanilla

Sift together flour, salt, and soda. Add shortening, sugars, egg, and vanilla. Beat until smooth. Fold in oats. Shape dough into rolls, wrap in waxed paper and chill thoroughly or freeze.

To cook: Slice ¼-inch thick and place on ungreased cookie sheet. Bake at 350 degrees for 10 minutes. Makes 4 dozen.

Note: You may add ¼ cup chopped nuts or ½ cup raisins to dough if desired.

--*Kitty Ellison*

MICROWAVE PEANUT BRITTLE

1 cup white sugar
½ cup white corn syrup
1/8 tsp. salt

1 cup raw peanuts
1 tsp. vanilla
1 tsp. soda

Mix first 4 ingredients in a large bowl. Microwave 4 minutes; stir and repeat for 4 minutes. Stir; add vanilla and butter. Stir and microwave 1½ to 2 minutes. Add baking soda. Stir and quickly pour onto a greased cookie sheet. Let it seek its own level; do not spread. Cool and break into serving pieces. Yummy!

--Marilyn McCaulley

And what could be better than preserves and butter on a toasted English muffin?

RHUBARB PRESERVES

5 cups diced rhubarb   3 cups sugar

Mix well and let stand overnight. Bring to a boil and cook 5 minutes. Add 1 small package strawberry jello. Stir well. Pour into sterilized jars. Freeze until ready to use. Thaw and serve. Makes 5 cups.

--Kitty Ellison

TRIPLE PEANUT COOKIES

½ cup shortening
½ cup peanut butter
½ cup brown sugar
1 cup sugar
1 tsp. vanilla

2 eggs
2 cups flour
1 tsp. baking soda
1 cup chopped unsalted peanuts
2 cups peanut butter chips

Cream shortening, peanut butter, and sugar. Add eggs and vanilla and beat well. Combine flour and soda; add to creamed mixture. Stir in chips and peanuts. Drop by teaspoons onto ungreased cookie sheet. Bake at 350 degrees for 10 to 12 minutes. Cool before removing from pan. Makes 5 dozen.

--Judy Coleman Bowden

Little toots need a good hearty breakfast before spending a day on the ski hill...that goes for mothers and fathers also!

GRANOLA BUBBLE RING

1½ cups granola
3/4 cup firmly packed brown
  sugar
1½ tsps. cinnamon
2 8-oz. pkgs. refrigerated
  biscuits

½ cup butter or margarine,
  melted
Additional raisins and/or
  nuts (optional)

Generously grease a 12-cup bundt pan. Combine granola, sugar, and cinnamon. Separate dough and cut each biscuit in half; dip in melted butter, then roll in the granola mixture coating generously and pressing into dough. Layer in bundt pan and sprinkle with remaining cereal and butter. Add additional raisins and nuts if desired. Bake at 350 degrees for 30 minutes; turn out immediately onto serving plate. Serve warm.

CHERRY CINNAMON WAFFLES

1-3/4 cups sifted flour
3 tsps. baking powder
2 Tbs. sugar
1 tsp. cinnamon
½ tsp. salt

1-3/4 cups milk
4 eggs, separated
½ cup cherry pie filling
1 cup whipping cream, whipped

Sift together the dry ingredients. Beat together milk, egg yolks, and butter; add to dry ingredients. Beat egg whites to soft peaks and fold into the batter. Bake according to waffle iron instructions.

Slowly heat the cherry pie filling and serve over waffles. Top with dollops of whipped cream. Serves 8.

Put this together the night before and serve it with the Granola Bubble Ring for a delightful company breakfast...

BACON AND EGG STRATA

2 cups soft bread crumbs
1-3/4 cups milk
8 slightly beaten eggs
Salt and pepper to taste
4 Tbs. butter
¼ tsp. seasoned salt

½ lb. sliced Swiss cheese
2 Tbs. butter
½ cup bread crumbs
8 slices bacon, cooked and
  crumbled

Soak the bread crumbs and milk until softened; drain through a strainer and reserve bread. Combine milk with eggs and seasonings. Melt the butter in a skillet and cook eggs until very soft stage but not fully cooked; stir in the reserved bread crumbs. Turn into a buttered 9-inch square baking pan. Sprinkle with seasoning salt and top with cheese. Combine the butter and bread crumbs with crumbled bacon and sprinkle over cheese. Bake at 450 degrees for 15 minutes or until hot and bubbly. Serves 6. *--Anne Severson*

COTTAGE PANCAKES

1 cup cream style cottage
  cheese
6 eggs
½ cup sifted flour

¼ tsp. salt
¼ cup oil
¼ cup milk
½ tsp. vanilla

Put all the ingredients in a blender and mix until creamy. Bake on hot griddle until nicely browned on each side. Serve with syrup or jelly. Serves 4.

--Maggie Subr

 APPLE CIDER SYRUP: Combine in saucepan ½ cup sugar, ¼ tsp. pumpkin-pie spice, 1 cup apple cider, 1 Tbs. lemon juice, 2 Tbs. currants, 2 Tbs. butter. Cook, stirring, until mixture thickens and boils for 1 minute. Serve over pancakes or hot bisuits. Makes 1½ cups.

Oh! to be a high school student in Steamboat Springs today
and to be a part of producing "Three Wire Winter." This
magazine is a credit to the school and the young men and
women who produce it. Inaugurated in the fall of 1975, it
covers personalities, places, and events in Routt County
history. The project was initially funded by the local Historical Society, the Arts and Humanities Council, Steamboat
Springs Bicentennial Committee, and the local school board.
Since 1976, however, it has been self supporting.

Perhaps the most difficult thing about producing Volume 1,
Number 1, was selecting a name. It took the 24 members more
than two weeks to decide on one. They yelled "Scratch" to
such names as Whistlepig and Magpie, and in desperation even
considered Cowpie. But the name THREE WIRE WINTER came to
them through local author Jean Wren. The term "Three Wire
Winter" means that the snow has come up to the third wire on
a barbed wire fence, thus indicating a severe season.

The students start the year with a training session, old members teaching new staffers the techniques of producing the
magazine. They are instructed in interviewing, photography,
darkroom use, sales, and distribution. But this is not the
only duty a staff member performs...one must raise money for
production. There is the annual seafood sale, a carnival
booth with an old-fashioned cake walk, and for fun a float is
designed for Homecoming parade.

Much of the history used in this cookbook was researched in
past issues of THREE WIRE WINTER. The students' dedication
to their subjects is evident and the creative style in which
the stories are written is a credit to their fertile imagination.

To renew or purchase a subscription (tax deductible):

    THREE WIRE WINTER
    Box 664
    Steamboat Springs, Colorado 80477

Have you ever seen a high school student who didn't thrive on pasta? Anne Severson, member of the cookbook committee, is noted for her pasta-making skill. She serves it up proudly to family and friends.

EGG PASTA

3 cups all-purpose flour	1 tsp. salt
4 eggs	1 to 2 Tbs. warm water
1 Tbs. olive oil	Flour

Insert steel blade. Place 3 cups flour, eggs, oil and salt in bowl; process until thoroughly blended, 3 to 5 seconds. With machine running, add 1 to 2 tablespoons warm water through feed tube; process until dough forms ball.

Once dough has formed ball, let dough spin around bowl 15 to 20 seconds.

Roll dough ball in flour. Cover with plastic wrap and let stand 30 minutes.

To roll by hand: Cut dough into 2 pieces. With a rolling pin, roll out and stretch one piece of dough on floured surface to thickness of a dime (keep other piece of dough sealed in plastic wrap). Flour dough as necessary to keep it from sticking. Cut into desired lengths or shapes.

If you are fortunate enough to own a pasta machine, use the manufacturer's directions.

--Anne Severson

PESTO SAUCE

2 large cloves garlic, peeled	2 tsp. salt
3 ozs. imported Parmesan cheese, room temperature, cut in 1-inch cubes	¼ cup pine nuts or walnuts
	1 cup oil (Anne prefers 3/4 cup safflower oil and ¼ cup olive oil combined)
2 cups fresh basil leaves or 2 cups Italian parsley leaves or spinach (2 Tbs. dried basil, firmly packed can be substituted)	

Food processor method: With the machine running, mince the

garlic by dropping it through the feed tube. Add the cheese and chop it by turning the machine on and off about 10 times. Add the basil, salt and nuts and mince them by turning on and off 8 times. With the machine running, drizzle the oil through the feed tube in a thin steady stream. Process until well blended. Serve over hot pasta. Makes enough for 6 servings.

NOTE: Sauce keeps for months if covered with a thin coat of oil and refrigerated. Can also be frozen in plastic ice cube trays. Transfer frozen cubes to an airtight bag and defrost in amounts needed. Serve over spaghetti, fettuccine or ravioli.

CHEESE RAVIOLI WITH PESTO SAUCE

Egg pasta
2 ozs. Parmesan cheese, cut into 1-inch cubes
1 lb. ricotta cheese
½ cup cottage cheese

2 eggs
1 tsp. chopped fresh parsley
1 small clove garlic
1/8 tsp. salt
Flour

Make egg pasta.
In your food processor bowl combine parsley, garlic and Parmesan cheese until finely grated. Add ricotta, cottage cheese, eggs and salt to bowl; process until combined using on/off method.
Roll egg pasta into a large sheet as directed. Place 1 heaping tsp. of cheese filling at 2-inch intervals on sheet of pasta. Cover with second sheet of pasta. Gently press down around mounds of filling. Using a fluted pastry wheel, cut into 2-inch squares. Or, using a round cookie cutter, cut dough into 2-inch circles. Seal edges with tines of fork. Place ravioli on dry towel. Let dry 1 hour. Turn ravioli over and let dry another hour.
Heat 6 quarts of water to boiling. Just before adding ravioli, add 2 Tbs. salt. Drop ravioli into boiling water. When water returns to a boil, cook uncovered until al dente, 3 to 5 minutes. Remove ravioli with a slotted spoon; drain well.
Place on a heated serving platter. Add sauce and toss gently. Sprinkle with Parmesan cheese and serve immediately.

--Anne Severson

MEATBALLS

1½ lb. ground beef
½ cup Progresso bread crumbs
¼ cup grated Parmesan cheese
1 tsp. basil
½ tsp. oregano

½ tsp. salt
Dash of black pepper
Dash of red pepper
1 garlic clove, minced
1 egg

Mix together all of the ingredients. Form into 2-inch balls. Brown in heavy sauce pot.

ITALIAN RED SAUCE

Saute in a large kettle (use same pot that meatballs were browned in):

3 Tbs. olive oil
½ cup chopped onion
1 clove garlic, minced
2 tsp. basil

1 tsp. oregano
2 bay leaves
2 tsp. salt

When onions are clear and very soft, add:

1 15-oz. can tomato puree
1 6-oz. can tomato paste
3 Tbs. dry red wine
1 cup freshly-chopped
   tomatoes

¼ tsp. sugar
Dash of black pepper
Dash of red pepper
2½ cups water

Turn the heat down and simmer 30 to 40 minutes, stirring occasionally. Add meatballs and simmer 30 minutes.

--Anne Severson

PESTO POTATOES: Toss sliced hot potatoes with the prepared pesto. Arrange in a casserole and dust with Parmesan cheese. Broil 3 or 4 minutes or until top is nicely browned.

MELON OR PEARS WITH PROSCIUTTO

1 cantaloupe, Persian melon OR   Lime wedges
4 ripe pears   Pepper
¼ to ½ lb. thinly sliced
   prosciutto

Peel, seed, and cut melon into wedges. If using pears,
remove cores and cut into wedges just before serving. For
each serving wrap 2 small wedges (4 pear wedges) individu-
ally with prosciutto. Serve with a knife and fork as a
first course with lime to squeeze over each serving if desired. Have a peppermill readily available so guests may
season to their own tastes.

JUMBO CHOCOLATE COOKIES

These cookies stay soft, moist and delicious!

1 cup shortening   3 squares unsweetened
2 cups light brown sugar   chocolate, melted
1 tsp. salt   2 eggs
1 tsp. baking soda   2½ cups flour, sifted
2 tsps. vanilla   1 cup sour milk*
                                 1 cup chopped nuts

Cream shortening and brown sugar together; blend in salt,
soda and vanilla. Add chocolate and mix well. Beat in eggs.
Add flour alternately with sour milk; stir in nuts. Chill
dough one hour or longer. Drop from tablespoon onto lightly
greased cookie sheets. Leave ample space between cookies as
they spread when baking. Bake at 375 degrees for 15 to 18
minutes or until lightly browned around edges. Cool and
store in tightly closed container. Makes 30 jumbo 3-inch
cookies. For smaller cookies, drop from teaspoon.

*To make sour milk: mix 1 tablespoon lemon juice or distilled
 white vinegar with one cup milk and let stand 5 minutes.

--*Christine McKelvie*

The Old Swimming Hole

Most of us have fond memories of a creek, river, or lake where we learned to swim, but Steamboat Springs had its own heated pool way back in 1885. A large wooden structure covered the hot springs behind the present swimming pool, making the luxury of a hot bath with temperatures hovering around 100 degrees readily available. Few towns could boast of such an accommodation.

After the Denver, Salt Lake and Pacific Railroad brought tourists to Steamboat in 1908, residents decided to spruce up the old bath house and created a swimming pool of great proportions. There was an outdoor pool made of natural stone measuring 110 x 190 feet and a warm pool indoors beckoned year 'round. There were eight smaller pools and all served the town until the mid '60's when they were torn down to make way for the modern pool now used. To delight the children and the young at heart, a Shoot The Tube winds its way down the hillside ending in a splash in the pool.

Nothing is quite as invigorating as a swim on a warm summer day. Make it a family affair and follow it with a sandwich supper served on the deck as the sun sinks behind your favorite mountain.

GIANT PIZZA SANDWICH

½ lb. Italian sausage
1 small onion, chopped
¼ cup green pepper, chopped
1 4-oz. can sliced mushrooms, drained
2 Tbs. sliced pimiento-stuffed olives

½ tsp. oregano
1 cup mozzarella cheese, shredded
2 13-oz. frozen cheese pizzas

Remove casings from sausage and crumble sausage into a large skillet; add onion, green pepper, mushrooms, 2 tablespoons sliced olives, and oregano. Cook over medium heat until meat is browned; stir in <u>half</u> the cheese.
To assemble: Place 1 pizza on lightly greased baking sheet,

cheese side up. Spoon sausage mixture over pizza; top with second pizza, cheese side down. Wrap sandwich securely in foil. Bake at 375 degrees for 15 minutes; remove foil and bake an additional 10 minutes. Sprinkle remaining cheese on top of sandwich; bake for 5 minutes longer. Garnish with additional sliced olives, if desired. Serves 6 to 8.

--Sue Hoffman
Carlisle, Pennsylvania

CHIPPED HAM BARBECUE SANDWICH

½ lb. chipped ham (have deli person chip or "shave" boiled ham into ultra-thin slices)
3/4 cup Sweet Pepper Chili Sauce (or commercial brand)

¼ cup catsup
4 sandwich or hamburger buns

Combine the first 3 ingredients in a large frying pan. Heat over medium heat, then simmer 10 minutes, stirring occasionally. Serve in toasted sandwich buns. Serves 4.

SWEET PEPPER CHILI SAUCE

Excellent condiment for sandwiches and hamburgers.

1½ cups sugar
25 tomatoes
6 medium onions
2 scant Tbs. salt

1½ cups vinegar
4 sweet peppers - red and green
½ box whole mixed spices for pickling

Scald, peel and cut tomatoes; dice onions and peppers. Tie whole spices in cheesecloth and combine with all other ingredients in a 6-quart pan. Simmer at least 3 hours, until thick. Pour into hot, sterile jars, leaving ½-inch headspace. Adjust caps and process in water-bath canner. Process for 15 minutes, adding 1 minute for each 1,000 feet above sea level.

--Susan O'Brien

PEACHY CROISSANT

1 3-oz. pkg. cream cheese, softened	6 large croissants
1 3-oz. pkg. bleu cheese, softened	3 ripe peaches
	16 to 18 strips bacon, crisp cooked
Heavy cream	Lettuce

Blend the cheeses together using a little heavy cream to lighten the mixture. Peel and coarsely chop the peaches and gently fold into the cheese. Slice croissants in half horizontally.

To assemble sandwich, spread bottom half of croissant with 2 tablespoons of the cheese mixture. Layer 3 strips of bacon, top with lettuce, and finish with top half of croissant.

NOTE: For a hot sandwich, leave off the lettuce and warm entire sandwich at 350 degrees for about 15 minutes or until croissants feel warm to touch. Add lettuce after heating if desired. Serves 6.

Thinly sliced pears may be used instead of peaches.

SANDWICH SURPRISE

Perfect sandwich for a bridge luncheon!

Make your favorite recipe for chicken, ham or crab salad; enough for 10 sandwiches.

20 thin slices of white bread	1 Tbs. lemon juice
Butter, softened	½ tsp. salt
12 ozs. cream cheese with chives, softened	1 Tbs. cream or milk
	1 2¼-oz. pkg. slivered almonds
3 egg yolks	

Prepare your salad mixture. Line cookie sheet with foil. Butter both sides of bread. Place one slice on foil, generously cover with salad and top with second slice of bread. Combine cream cheese, yolks, lemon juice, salt and milk to soften. Ice the top and sides of sandwich as you would a cake. Cover with foil and seal. Refrigerate 24 hours. Uncover and let stand at room temperature before baking. Bake

about 30 minutes at 350 degrees or until golden brown.
Sprinkle with almonds the last 15 minutes of baking time.
Serves 10.

NOTE: Sandwiches are prettier if you use a round loaf of
bread or cut slices in rounds using a bowl as your
guide. Garnish with pimiento "flowers" and leaves of
parsley.

ROQUEFORT TOPPED CHICKEN SANDWICH

1 slice toasted white bread, trimmed	2½ ozs. sliced breast of chicken
Mayonnaise	Thin slices of tomato

Butter bottom of toast and place in ramekin dish, buttered
side down. Spread toast with mayonnaise; top with chicken
slice then tomato. Completely cover sandwich with Roquefort
Topping. Bake at 350 degrees for 20 minutes or until bubbly
and golden brown.

Roquefort Topping:

8 ozs. Roquefort cheese	1 egg
4 ozs. cream cheese with chives, room temperature	3/4 tsp. Worcestershire sauce
	½ tsp. Tabasco sauce

Beat in mixer until light and fluffy.

A marvelous accompaniment to any sandwich, hot or cold...

CHEESE POTATO CASSEROLE

2 12-oz. pkgs. frozen, hashed brown potatoes	1 Tbs. minced onion
2 cups sour cream	2 cups Cheddar cheese, shredded
1 can cream of chicken soup	2 cups coarsely crushed corn flakes
½ cup butter, melted	¼ cup melted butter
1 tsp. salt	

Place potatoes in colander, let stand until completely thawed
and excess moisture has drained off. Combine sour cream,
soup, and butter. Mix well. Add salt, onion and cheese. Mix
well. Blend in potatoes. Place in shallow 2-quart casserole.

Combine butter and corn flakes and sprinkle on top. Bake, uncovered, at 350 degrees about 50 minutes or until golden brown and bubbly. This is at its best when assembled not more than 2 hours before it goes into the oven. Serves 8.

--*Jan Vail*

SUMMER PEAR PIE

Cheese pastry and faintly spiced pears - an unsurpassable flavor team.

Cheese pastry for 2-crust pie
4 cups sliced peeled pears
1/3 cup granulated sugar
1/3 cup brown sugar, firmly
  packed

2 Tbs. cornstarch
¼ tsp. salt
¼ tsp. mace
2 Tbs. butter or margarine

Sprinkle lemon juice over pears. Combine sugars, cornstarch, salt and mace.
Place half of pears in pastry-lined 9-inch pie pan. Sprinkle with half the sugar mixture. Add remaining pears; sprinkle with remaining sugar mixture. Dot with butter. Adjust top crust; flute edges and cut vents.
Bake in 425 degree oven 35 to 40 minutes, or until pears are tender, crust is browned and juices bubble in vents.

CHEESE PASTRY

Marvelous for apple and many kinds of pies.

1-2/3 cups sifted flour
½ tsp. salt
1 cup grated sharp natural
  Cheddar cheese

½ cup vegetable shortening
4 to 6 Tbs. cold water

Sift flour with salt into medium bowl. Add cheese and toss with a fork to mix thoroughly with flour. Cut in shortening until mixture resembles small peas.
Sprinkle water over pastry mixture, 1 Tbs. at a time, until dough will hold together. Shape into a ball with hands, wrap in waxed paper and refrigerate until ready to use. Divide in halves, flatten each half with hand. Make bottom and top crusts. Makes pastry for 1 2-crust pie.

--*Mae Bryant*

Buddy Werner Memorial Library

Buddy Werner Memorial Library

There were many before and there will be many to come, but
it's unlikely that any will have the impact on a community
that Buddy Werner had on Steamboat Springs. He was a home-
town boy, everyone's friend, and he was a winner. Through
his skiing and winning he brought excitement and fame to
the mountain. And the town will never forget.

When Buddy was killed in April of 1964 while filming a ski
movie in Val Selin, Switzerland, Steamboat wanted to do something very special. It was decided that a library bearing
his name would be a worthy and a fitting memorial. Today
the tribute stands on the banks of the Yampa River east of
town. Its soaring roof and tall windows seem to reach for
the mountaintop...the mountaintop he so dearly loved. Inside one will find a display of pictures and memorabilia
surrounding Buddy's life.

Buddy was not the only skiing Werner, nor was he the only Werner champion. Skeeter Werner, a member of the 1956 Olympic ski team, and Loris Werner represented the U.S. in the '68 Olympics in Grenoble. They both make their homes near the mountain named for their brother.

Spending the morning in a library on a rainy or snowy day puts one in the mood to curl up before a fire with a good book. Household chores are set aside and pampering oneself with "goodies" just seems to be the thing to do...

SEVEN LAYER BARS

½ cup butter or margarine
1½ cups Graham cracker crumbs
1-1/3 cups coconut
2 cups peanut butter chips

1 cup raisins or semi-sweet chocolate chips
1 cup chopped walnuts
1 14-oz. can sweetened condensed milk

Place butter in a 13 x 9 x 12-inch baking dish and put in a warm oven until butter melts. Remove and sprinkle Graham cracker crumbs over butter. Press down slightly. Layer coconut, peanut butter chips, raisins or chocolate chips (or a combination) over the crumbs. Drizzle surface with the sweetened condensed milk. Bake at 350 degrees for 20 minutes or until lightly browned. Cut in bars to serve.

Hazie and Skeeter Werner

CARAMEL CORN

1 cup butter
2 cups brown sugar
½ cup Karo syrup
1 tsp. vanilla

½ tsp. soda
½ tsp. salt
6 quarts popped corn

Bring butter, sugar, syrup and salt to a boil, stirring constantly. Let boil for 5 minutes without stirring. Remove from heat and add vanilla and soda. Pour mixture over the popped corn and mix well. Bake in a 250 degree oven for 1 hour, stirring every 15 minutes.

--Lori Shelton

BANANA CAKE

1 or 2 ripe bananas	4 eggs
1 pkg. yellow cake mix	1 cup water
1 pkg. vanilla pudding or	½ cup oil
Banana Jello	½ cup chopped nuts

Mix well to directions on cake mix package. Pour into a well greased and floured tube pan and bake at 350 degrees for 60 to 70 minutes.

--Anne Stettner

SPICED COFFEE

1 cup regular-grind coffee	10 whole cloves
6 cubes sugar	3 cinnamon sticks
8 whole allspice	

Place the ingredients in the coffee percolator basket; use 6 cups water for perking. Serves 6 to 8.

Now that you have indulged yourself and pangs of guilt are creeping in, fly into the kitchen and whip up a special treat for the family...

STOVE TOP BEANS AND MEATBALLS

1 lb. lean ground beef	1 tsp. salt
½ cup evaporated milk	1/8 tsp. pepper
2/3 cup soft bread crumbs	

Combine the above and (with wet hands) shape into 16 meatballs. Brown in skillet with:

1 Tbs. shortening	1 cup sliced onion

Cover and cook over low heat for 10 minutes. Add:

1 16-oz. can pork and beans	2 Tbs. catsup
Dash of salt	¼ tsp. dry mustard

Cover and heat until bubbly. Serves 4.

--Betty Christoff

BASQUE PICKLED BEANS

1 lb. small white beans	1¼ cups salad oil
½ cup finely minced onion	1 tsp. salt
2 cloves garlic, crushed	½ tsp. fresh coarsely ground
¼ cup finely chopped fresh	pepper
parsley	¼ tsp. dried oregano, crushed
3/4 cup red wine vinegar	

In a 3-4 quart covered saucepan, soak the beans overnight in about 8 cups of cold water. After soaking, drain and return the beans to the saucepan with 2½ quarts fresh water. Cook until tender, about 1½ hours. Rinse the beans well with cool water and drain. While the beans are cooking, make a marinade by mixing the rest of the ingredients together in a small bowl. Pour the marinade over the warm beans. Stir well, cover, and chill at least 6 hours. Serves 8.

Note: This is an excellent addition to an antipasto tray.

CHOCOLATE OATMEAL CAKE

1 cup rolled oats	1 cup sifted flour
1½ cups boiling water	½ cup cocoa
½ cup shortening	1 tsp. soda
1½ cups sugar	½ tsp. salt
2 eggs	1 tsp. vanilla

Mix oats and boiling water together; let cool. Cream shortening with sugar and eggs. Add cooled oatmeal mixture alternately with flour, soda, cocoa, and salt. Stir in vanilla. Pour into a greased and floured 13 x 9 x 2-inch baking dish and bake at 350 degrees for 30 minutes or until cake tests done. Frost with Cocoa Nut Frosting.

Cocoa Nut Frosting:

1 cup powdered sugar	2 Tbs. butter
2 cups coconut	½ cup milk

Combine in a saucepan and boil until thickened. Spread on cooled cake. Serves 10 to 12.

--Hazie Werner

7-83

The Old Depot

Rock from the Emerald Mountain quarry was used to build the Steamboat Springs Depot, now listed on the National Register of Historic Places. The depot was built through the efforts of 1,200 stalwart citizens who raised $15,000 to guarantee the arrival of the Moffat Road in 1909. Even before it was completed, the town gave a rousing welcome to David Moffat, who arrived in his private railway coach on the first passenger train into Steamboat. This coach now houses the Craig Chamber of Commerce and makes an interesting "side trip" for visitors to the area.

During those early years the rail trip from Denver to Steamboat took 12 hours...if the weather was good; snow often stranded the train, extending the trip to as long as three days. Once passengers arrived in Steamboat they could hire a taxi to any place in town for 25¢.

No longer is there the romance of traveling by rail across the mountains from Denver to Steamboat; but there is romance of a different kind. The Steamboat Springs Council of the Arts and Humanities has leased, remodeled, and is using the

building as a community and arts center. Now the rafters
ring with actors' on-stage voices and the applause of
approving audiences. Deserving artists of the community are
provided a showcase for their work. The Depot at Steamboat
Springs has come full circle, thanks to those early citizens
who built it and to the present ones who are sustaining it
for all to enjoy.

*You too can become a "deserving artist." Paint a canvas of
beautiful foods to serve delighted dinner guests. End it
with your most serious work of art, a Molded French Cream
demanding rave reviews.*

CURRY VEGETABLE DIP

Combine 1 cup mayonnaise or salad dressing with 1 tsp. tarragon vinegar, 1 tsp. horseradish, and 2 to 3 tsps. curry
powder. Mix well and use as a dip for fresh vegetables.
Makes 1 cup.

--Susie Baker, an artist

SPINACH SOUP

1 10-oz. pkg. frozen spinach	½ tsp. pepper
½ cup sliced onions	¼ tsp. nutmeg
2 Tbs. butter	3 egg yolks
1 potato, sliced	½ cup half and half
4 cups chicken stock	¼ cup sauterne
1½ tsps. salt	1 tsp. lemon juice

Thaw spinach. Saute onions in butter; add spinach and cook
5 minutes. Add stock, potato, salt and pepper. Simmer 20
to 30 minutes. Cool. Puree in a blender in small batches.
Put back in pot and bring to a simmer. Mix cream and egg
yolks and stir in a little of the hot soup; add all to the
soup. Add sauterne and lemon juice. Heat gently and don't
let it boil or it will curdle. This is good hot or cold.
Serves 6 to 8.

--Maureen Keefner

HAM WITH GREEN GRAPE SAUCE

3 to 4 lb. ham with bone
1 small onion, diced
1 tsp. each, marjoram,
   rosemary, bay leaf, and
   parsley

10 peppercorns
1 Tbs. tarragon

Put the ham, onion, and carrots in a large pot and cover with water. Combine the remaining ingredients and tie in a cheese-cloth bag; add to pot. Simmer, covered, for 20 minutes per pound. Serve sliced with the sauce.

Green Grape Sauce:

3/4 cup sauterne
1 Tbs. finely chopped onion
3 egg yolks, room temperature
Salt and white pepper to taste
2 Tbs. butter
2 Tbs. flour

1½ cups heated chicken stock
1/3 cup warmed half and half
Lemon juice (optional)
1 lb. green grapes, halved
   (room temperature)

Combine wine and onion and boil, reducing to ¼ cup when strained. Beat egg yolks until light in color. Put in a pan over simmering water and gradually add the sauterne, the butter, salt and pepper. Stir constantly until thickened (add another egg yolk if mixture separates). Set aside.

In a heavy saucepan melt 2 Tbs. butter until bubbly, whisk in flour and cook on low for 1 to 2 minutes, stirring con-stantly. Gradually add chicken stock, whisking until thick. Add half and half, salt and pepper to taste, and lemon juice. Add to the sauterne mixture. Fold in the grapes and serve over ham.

--Maureen Keefner

 CRISPY CARROTS: Melt ½ stick butter in a large skillet; add 1¼ cups finely chopped onion and cook until tender. Blend in 2 Tbs. brown sugar and 1¼ tsp. salt. Add 2 cups coarsely shredded carrots. Toss lightly and cook until crisp but tender, only about 5 minutes. Sprinkle with chopped fresh parsley to serve. Serves 4 to 6.

BRUSSELS SPROUTS WITH PECAN BUTTER TOPPING

1½ lbs. Brussel sprouts
Salted water
1/3 cup chicken stock
2 Tbs. chopped onion
½ tsp. salt

½ cup sliced or chopped pecans
¼ cup butter or margarine
Pimiento strips
Parsley

Trim the Brussel sprouts and soak in salted water to cover
for about 20 minutes. Drain and rinse with cold water. In a
sauce pan bring the chicken stock to a boil; add the sprouts,
onions and salt. Cook uncovered for 5 minutes; cover and
cook 10 minutes longer or until sprouts are tender but
lightly crisp. Drain, if necessary, and keep hot. Saute
pecans in butter for 2 to 3 minutes until golden brown. Pour
mixture over sprouts and mix lightly. Garnish with pimiento
and sprigs of parsley. Serves 6.

--Cookbook Committee

MOLDED FRENCH CREAM

1 cup heavy cream
1 cup sour cream
3/4 cup granulated sugar
1 envelope Knox gelatin

¼ cup water
1 8-oz. pkg. cream cheese,
   softened
½ tsp. vanilla

Brush a 4-cup mold lightly with oil. Combine sour cream and
cream in a saucepan, beat in sugar and place over low heat.
Sprinkle gelatin in water to soften; add to cream mixture,
stir 1 minute and remove from heat.
Beat cream cheese until soft and smooth, add vanilla and
gradually stir in the cream mixture. Pour into the prepared
mold and refrigerate at least 4 hours. Unmold on serving
plate. Pour sauce over just before serving.

Raspberry Sauce:

1 carton frozen raspberries,
   thawed

2 Tbs. Kirsch
¼ cup powdered sugar

Puree raspberries and strain seeds out. Mix in remaining
ingredients and stir. Serves 8.

--Maureen Keefner

LIBBY RUSSELL - ARTIST

Libby (Elizabeth Jean) Russell is a sophomore art history major at Colorado College in Colorado Springs. She has donated her time and talents to the Hospital Auxiliary by sketching major points of interest in the town where she grew up. They grace the pages of this cookbook.

Libby is 20 years of age and attended high school at the Putney School in Vermont and graduated, cum laude, from the Foxcroft School in Middleburg, Virginia. She served for two years as an intern with the Metropolitan Museum of Art in New York City and will further her art studies next year in England and Italy under the foreign student program at Colorado College.

Jean and Dick Russell, Libby's proud parents, were one of the first couples to live at the new ski area and later made their home in Strawberry Park. Jean edited "Steamboat Simmers" in 1972, little realizing that her young daughter would eventually illustrate the second edition.

ALMOND TOPPED CHEESE CAKE *"A work of art."*

3 8-oz. pkgs. cream cheese, softened
4 egg whites
1 cup sugar
1 tsp. vanilla
2/3 cup Zwieback, crushed
2 cups sour cream
2 Tbs. sugar
½ tsp. vanilla
1/3 cup toasted, blanched almonds

Cream the cheese until fluffy. Beat the egg whites until stiff; beat in the sugar. Combine cream cheese and egg white mixtures; add vanilla. Pour into a 3-inch deep spring-form pan which has been buttered and dusted with the crushed Zwieback. Bake at 350 degrees for 25 minutes.

Combine sour cream, sugar and remaining vanilla. Remove cake from oven and spread mixture over the top; sprinkle with almonds. Increase heat to 475 degrees and cook for 5 minutes. Chill at least 2 hours before serving. Serves 6.

--Jean Russell

"Tread of Pioneers" Museum
Founded June 1959

Tread Of Pioneers Museum

"I hear the tread of pioneers, of nations yet to be, the first low wash of waves, where soon shall roll a human sea."
--Whittier

Located at Fifth and Oak Streets is a small frame cottage dating from the early part of the century and housing memories of the tread of pioneers to Routt County. Since its beginning in 1959 the museum has been located in its present building. Volunteers serve as guides and curators from Memorial Day to Labor Day. One should plan to spend several hours to fully absorb the treasured past.

Many of the artifacts in the museum belonged to Lillian Crawford, the first white child born in the valley. A graceful rosewood piano, purchased in New York and shipped around the Horn to California as a birthday present, dominates one room. There are elegant gowns, men's formal attire, and a charming little niche dedicated to children. The basement houses an outstanding Indian collection while the Mineral Room tells the story of mining in this area.

The Ski Room is particularly interesting. Wide wooden boards of torture with leather straps from the early days...only the very dexterous could possibly have handled the skis mounted on these walls. There are trophies of Carl Howelsen, skis of Gordy Wren and Buddy Werner, and memorabilia covering the glorious history of skiing in Steamboat.

Heavy cast iron pots adorn a wood stove in the kitchen. The walls are hung with a treasure trove of antique kitchen utensils giving one reason to stop and ponder over how our grandmothers managed to produce the hearty meals needed to sustain their families. But linger a while, close your eyes, and you can just smell the hunter's stew bubbling on the stove and the hot bread and cookies baking in the oven...

FRUITED VENISON STEW

1½ lbs. venison chuck roast
   cut in 2-inch cubes
2 tsps. Kitchen Bouquet
2 tsps. salt
Dash of pepper
¼ cup cooking oil
1 small onion, diced
2 beef bouillon cubes

2 cups hot water
2 Tbs. brown sugar
1 Tbs. lemon juice
16 large prunes, pitted
4 medium carrots, cut in
   1-inch pieces
4 medium potatoes, cut in
   1-inch pieces

Place meat in mixing bowl; sprinkle with Kitchen Bouquet, 1
tsp. salt and pepper. Toss to coat. Heat oil in heavy
saucepan; add meat and brown quickly. Add onion and cook for
2 minutes, stirring constantly. Combine bouillon cubes,
water, brown sugar and lemon juice; add to meat.

Cover, bring to a boil and simmer about 1 hour or until
tender; add water if needed. Add prunes, remaining salt,
carrots and potatoes. Cook 30 minutes longer or until vegetables are tender. Serves 6.

--*Joanna Smith*

BOSTON COOKIES

*From the kitchen of Mrs. Lulie M. Pritchett, the oldest
daughter of James H. Crawford who founded the town of Steamboat Springs. Her 1885 homesteading experiences are des-
cribed by her daughter in "Cabin at Medicine Springs."*

1 cup butter
1½ cups sugar
3 eggs, beaten
1 tsp. soda
1½ Tbs. hot water
3¼ cups flour

½ tsp. salt
1 tsp. cinnamon
1 cup chopped English walnuts
½ cup raisins
½ cup currants

Combine the butter and sugar and beat well; beat in eggs.
Dissolve the soda in the hot water; add to mixture. Sift
together the flour, salt, and cinnamon. Add half of this to
the butter mixture; stir in walnuts, raisins, and currants.
Add the remaining flour mixture and stir to form a stiff

dough. Drop by spoonfuls, 1-inch apart, on a buttered cookie
sheet. Bake at 350 degrees until nicely browned, about 12
minutes.

WALTER'S BISCUITS

2 cups flour
4 tsps. baking powder
1 tsp. salt
½ tsp. cream of tartar

1 Tbs. sugar
2/3 cup Crisco shortening
2/3 cup milk

Combine all ingredients. Pat or roll on floured board to ½-
inch thickness. Cut with biscuit cutter to desired size.
Bake at 450 degrees for 10 to 12 minutes or until nicely
browned.

--Walter Verhalen
Dallas, Texas

HERMITS

*From the kitchen of Ellen Groesbeck, wife of the first post-
master to manage the downtown post office.*

2 cups sugar
1 cup butter
1 cup raisins, chopped
1 cup flour
3 eggs

½ cup milk with ½ tsp. soda
  dissolved in it
1 tsp. each, cinnamon, cloves
  and nutmeg

Combine ingredients and mix well. Drop from a teaspoon onto
a greased cookie sheet. Bake at 350 degrees until lightly
browned.

SPICED TEA: Steep ¼ cup Pekoe tea, 1 cinnamon stock, ½ Tbs.
             whole allspice in 2 cups boiling water for 1
hour. Strain and add 1 cup sugar, ½ cup orange juice, ½ cup
lemon juice, enough water to make ½ gallon of liquid. Good
hot or cold. Makes 20 cups.

*From the kitchen of Mrs. Archie Wither, wife of the owner of
one of the area's earliest mercantile stores, located first
at Hahns Peak, then in Steamboat across from the present
courthouse.*

A "Dandy" Cereal

Yampa Valley Milling and Elevator Company was opened just east of Steamboat Springs in 1890. Farmers had an outlet for their wheat, homemakers made use of Yampa Valley flour, the economy experienced an upswing, and a new cereal was introduced to area youngsters. The cereal was named "Joe Dandy" when rancher Joe Lewis tasted the wheat cereal and pronounced it just "dandy." The secret formula was handed down from miller to miller over the years but production was discontinued when local prices could no longer compete with those of flour imported from Denver.

What would the modern homemaker do without cereal? It is a breakfast mainstay, afternoon or late night snack, and is "just dandy" in the recipes to follow...

MAPLE BRAN MUFFINS

3/4 cup sugar
¼ cup oil
1¼ cups raisin bran
1 egg
1 cup buttermilk

1¼ cups flour
1½ tsps. baking soda
½ tsp. salt
4 Tbs. maple syrup
4 Tbs. chopped nuts
  (optional)

Preheat oven to 400 degrees. Grease muffin tins or line with paper liners. Combine ingredients in order listed; stir to blend but do not beat. Pour into prepared tins and bake for 20 minutes. Makes 12 muffins.

RICE KRISPIES DESSERT

1 cup sugar
1 cup light corn syrup
1 cup peanut butter
6 cups rice krispies

1 6-oz. pkg. chocolate chips
1 6-oz. pkg. butterscotch
chips

Combine sugar and syrup and cook to bubbling; remove from heat and stir in peanut butter and rice krispies. Pat into a buttered 9 x 13-inch pan. Melt the chocolate and butterscotch

chips (microwave is great for this!) over low heat. Pour
over rice krispies, spread evenly. Let cool before cutting
into squares.

--*Joyce Taylor*

*Oatmeal is a favorite hot cereal in most households but should
not always be cooked and served with cream and sugar...it has
many uses!*

OATMEAL-DATE PIE

My children loved this pie for breakfast!

1/5 cup soft butter or margarine	1¼ cups regular or quick-cooking oatmeal
1 cup honey	3/4 cup pitted dates, snipped
3 eggs	1 9-inch unbaked pie shell
1/8 tsp. salt	Vanilla ice cream (optional)
1 tsp. vanilla	

Beat the butter and honey until creamy; add the eggs and beat
until smooth. Stir in the salt, vanilla, rolled oats, and
dates. Pour the date mixture into the prepared pie shell and
bake at 350 degrees for 45 minutes or until center is set
when touched. Let cool completely before cutting. Top each
serving with vanilla ice cream if desired.

--*Regina Hollberg*
Englewood, Colorado

OATMEAL CHOCOLATE CHIP CAKE

1-3/4 cup boiling water	1-3/4 cup flour
1 cup uncooked oatmeal	1 tsp. soda
1 cup lightly packed brown sugar	1 12-oz. pkg. semi-sweet chocolate chips
1 cup granulated sugar	3/4 cup chopped walnuts or pecans
½ cup margarine	
2 extra large eggs	

Pour boiling water over oatmeal. Let stand 10 minutes at
room temperature. Add sugars and margarine. Stir until margarine melts. Add eggs and mix well. Sift together the dry
ingredients and combine with the oatmeal mixture; mix well.
Stir in half of the chocolate chips. Pour cake mixture into

65

a greased and floured 9 x 13-inch pan; sprinkle chopped nuts
and remaining chocolate chips on top. Bake at 350 degrees
for about 40 minutes or until a wooden pick comes out clean.
After cake has cooled, lightly sprinkle with powdered sugar.

--Jan Vail

*Another staple in most households is potato chips. They are
used to munch on, top casserole dishes, a dipper for dips,
and in cookies...yes, cookies! One is for the sweet tooth
and the other to serve with soups, salads, or cocktails.*

MR. CHIPS COOKIES

1 cup butter or margarine
½ cup sugar
½ cup crushed potato chips

½ cup chopped pecans
2 cups sifted flour
1 tsp. vanilla

Mix all the ingredients and form into small balls. Press
flat with bottom of glass dipped in sugar. Bake 16 to 18
minutes at 350 degrees on an ungreased cookie sheet. Do not
let them get overly browned...just golden in color. Makes
2 dozen.

--Dee Richards

CHIPPER CHEDDARS

¼ cup butter or margarine,
  melted
1-1/3 cups cheddar cheese,
  grated
1 cup finely crushed potato
  chips

½ cup sifted flour
Pinch of dry mustard
Generous dash of cayenne
  pepper
Parmesan cheese (optional)

Preheat oven to 450 degrees and lightly grease a cookie
sheet. Combine all ingredients except Parmesan cheese. Roll
heaping teaspoons of mixture into balls and arrange on baking
sheet. Flatten with the tines of a fork. Lightly sprinkle
with Parmesan cheese. Bake until crisp and golden brown 12
to 15 minutes (do not underbake or they will not be crisp).
Store in airtight containers or freeze for later use...if
they last! Makes 2 dozen.

Charles "Chuck" Leckenby indeed has printer's ink in his blood. His grandfather bought the STEAMBOAT PILOT in 1896 and his father, Maurice, was born above the print shop. Maurice continued the tradition of good newspapering and during his years as editor won awards for outstanding editor and general excellence. He was named Democratic State Chairman and continued the family interest in politics.

It was because of Maurice's preoccupation with political activities in Washington D.C. that Chuck moved to Steamboat to take charge of the Pilot. At the time, his college friends thought he was burying himself in an isolated small town. Now, with the popular ski area, they are all frequent visitors.

Chuck is fond of saying that he worked his way up from janitor. True to the newspaper blood in his family, he was graduated with honors in journalism from the University of Colorado. He was on the ski team for four years and was a skiing companion and competitor with other Steamboat greats...Buddy Werner, Marvin Crawford, and Keith Wegeman.

It was while Chuck was serving in the Air Force that he met Nancy Gordon, a journalism student at the University of Idaho. They were married in 1957 and returned to Steamboat. Since that time Chuck has acted as editor of the Pilot. He has expanded and improved the newspaper and won several awards for outstanding editorials. Nancy writes a weekly column for the Pilot, FROM THE BOILER ROOM, a controversial and candid comment on daily life.

"The Boiler Room" might describe the way some women feel about their kitchens...not so Nancy Leckenby. She enjoys cooking for her children and entertaining in her home. Her recipe for Kahlua is one to enjoy and would make a beautiful Christmas present bottled and tied with a satin bow.

NANCY'S KAHLUA

Boil 4 cups water and 4 cups sugar for 5 minutes. Add 3/4 cup instant coffee to make a paste. Bring to a boil; remove from heat and cool. Add 1/5 quart bourbon. Cut a vanilla bean into 1-inch pieces and add. Cover. After one week taste occasionally and remove vanilla bean only when flavor suits you (up to 2 weeks). Pour in bottles and keep in a cool place.

Never drink more than one -- the Voice of Experience!

Making your own liqueur can be a marvelous way to dazzle your guest. Serve it chilled as an after-dinner drink or use it as the main ingredient in spectacular desserts...

KAHLUA MOUSSE

½ cup sugar
½ cup water
2 eggs
1 6-oz. pkg. chocolate chips
2 Tbs. brandy

3 Tbs. kahlua
1 cup whipping cream, whipped
Grated chocolate
Toasted slivered almonds

Heat sugar in water until dissolved; set aside. Mix eggs, salt and chocolate in blender. Add sugar mixture slowly and blend until thick. Cool. Add brandy and kahlua. Fold half the whipped cream into the chocolate mixture. Chill several hours and serve in small wine glasses. Top with remaining cream and sprinkle with grated chocolate and slivered almonds. Serves 6.

RASPBERRY OR STRAWBERRY LIQUEUR

1½ lbs. (3½ cups) sugar
24 ozs. vodka

1½ lbs. crushed strawberries
or raspberries.

Combine sugar and vodka and whisk until sugar is almost dis-solved. Add the crushed berries and put in a large 1-gallon bottle with a tight lid. Shake jar gently once daily until fruit sinks to the bottom, 4 weeks or more. Strain through a clean gauze or nylon. Pour into bottles and cap. Makes 1 quart.

--Leona Littlefield

RASPBERRY OR STRAWBERRY SORBET

2 cups simple syrup (recipe below)
4 cups berries, cleaned, drained and hulled
2 Tbs. raspberry or strawberry liqueur
Juice of ½ lemon

Make the simple syrup. Puree berries in a food processor. Press puree through a medium sieve. Stir in syrup, liqueur and lemon juice. Pour in freezer trays and freeze until almost solid; remove and whip until fluffy. Put back into trays and freeze. Remove from freezer about 1 hour before serving.

Simple Syrup:

2 cups sugar
2 cups water

Combine and bring to a boil; reduce heat and simmer 5 minutes. Cool to room temperature.

NOTE: 2 Tbs. Framboise may be used if you haven't made your own liqueur.

--Leona Littlefield

COMPANY CHICKEN

4 Tbs. butter
Garlic powder
6 chicken breasts
1 tsp. salt
Pepper to taste
½ lb. sliced mushrooms
1 3-oz. can fried onion rings
½ cup grated white cheese

Melt butter or margarine in a casserole dish and add garlic powder to taste. Dredge chicken in flour and dip in the seasoned butter. Place skin side down in a flat baking dish. Bake for 30 minutes at 425 degrees; turn chicken and bake another 30 minutes. Drain chicken drippings into a small skillet and saute mushrooms for several minutes then put them on top of the chicken. Sprinkle with cheese and onion rings and return to oven until cheese melts.

Microwave Directions: Bake the chicken as directed. Slice mushrooms into a small dish and cover with the chicken drippings. Cover with Saran and microwave for 3 minutes. Continue with directions as given.

--Dee Richards

BLACK BOTTOM CUPCAKES

1 cup cream cheese
1 egg
1/3 cup sugar
1/8 tsp. salt
1 8-oz. pkg. chocolate chips
1½ cups flour
1 cup sugar

1 tsp. soda
½ tsp. salt
1 cup water
1/3 cup cooking oil
1 Tbs. vinegar
1 tsp. vanilla
Sugar and chopped almonds

Combine the cream cheese, egg, sugar, and salt. Beat well and stir in the chocolate chips. Set aside. Sift together the dry ingredients and add the water, oil, vinegar and vanilla. Beat well. Line muffin tins with paper liners and fill cups to 1/3 with flour mixture. Top each with a heaping teaspoon of cream cheese mixture; sprinkle with sugar and chopped blanched almonds. Bake at 350 degrees for 30 to 35 minutes. Refrigerate before serving. Makes 2 dozen.

--Nancy Leckenby

This would make a very newsworthy dish for any family supper.

IMPOSSIBLE REUBEN PIE

1 8-oz. can sauerkraut,
    drain and press out all
    liquid
½ lb. cooked corned beef,
    diced medium-fine
    (about 1½ cups)
4 ozs. Swiss cheese, shredded
    (equals 1 cup packed)

1 cup milk
3/4 cup biscuit mix
1/3 cup mayonnaise
2 Tbs. chili sauce
3 large eggs

Drain the sauerkraut and press out liquid; there should be ½ cup of kraut. Sprinkle the bottom of a buttered, clear glass 9 x 1¼-inch pie plate with the chopped corn beef. Top with cheese, then the kraut.

In a blender, at high speed, whir the the remaining five ingredients about 15 seconds. Pour over the mixture in the pie plate...do not stir. Bake at 400 degrees until bottom and sides are well browned and top is golden, about 30 minutes. Let stand about 5 minutes and serve at once. Serves 6.

Colorado's Brooklyn

In the early 1900's the Steamboat Springs Town Company prohibited the making and sale of liquor, thereby creating a situation most unpopular with the many cowboys who frequented the area. However, high spirits will out, and a group of enterprising people crossed to the west side of the Yampa River and created a town called Brooklyn for the sole purpose of fun.

The town consisted of four blocks of rollicking saloons, houses of ill repute, and pool halls overflowing with traveling salesmen, cowboys, and curious adventurers. Business was booming! Shorty Anderson's, Fred Cheetel's, and The Capitol were the leading saloons where no women were allowed to enter. Then there was Hazel McGuire's where liquor and anything else your heart desired was served.

Most of the women of the area had their own house or room. There was no electricity so red lanterns were hung over the windows or doors as symbols of their trade. Despite the wild, wild women and the aura of sin surrounding the area, residents from near and far crossed the river to Brooklyn where they made camp during the rodeo and Strawberry Festival celebrations.

A Brooklyn-days costume party would be great fun. Ask your guests to come dressed depicting the early times in Brooklyn, decorate your tables with red lanterns, dance 'til the wee hours of the morning, and don't forget to serve a sumptious buffet to your cowboys and madams...

BROOKLYN BLOOMER DROPPERS

1 6-oz. can frozen limeade	1 pkg. frozen strawberries
1 tsp. sugar	2 cups ice cubes
1 egg white	6 ozs. rum (more if desired)

Blend until thickened. Serve with a whole berry on the edge of a pretty wine or brandy glass. Serves 4.

--Joanna Smith

STUFFED MUSHROOMS

1 cup grated Parmesan cheese
20 green olives, chopped
2 Tbs. dry minced onion

6 strips bacon, crisp fried
  and crumbled
3/4 cup mayonnaise
6 dozen large mushroom caps

Combine all the ingredients except mushrooms and blend well. Clean the mushroom caps and stuff with the cheese mixture. Broil for 5 minutes. Makes 72; recipe can be cut in half if desired.

--Newell Campbell

CITRUS CHICKEN

3 boned chicken breasts,
  halved
¼ cup melted butter or
  margarine
1 Tbs. orange liqueur
6 thin slices cooked ham
Flour
2 slightly beaten eggs

1 stick butter, cut in bits
2 cups fresh orange juice
1 tsp. orange peel, grated
1 Tbs. tarragon
½ tsp. salt
6 ½-inch slices orange,
  orange peel and finely
  minced parsley

Preheat oven to 400 degrees. Flatten chicken breasts with a mallet or knife handle and brush with the melted butter mixed with orange liqueur. Place 1 slice of ham on each chicken breast and roll up, securing with a toothpick. Roll in flour; shake off excess. Dip rolls in beaten egg, then in crumbs. Arrange in a 12 x 8 x 2-inch pan. Dot with butter. Bake 15 minutes; turn. Combine orange juice, tarragon, peel and salt and pour over chicken. Reduce oven temperature to 350 degrees, cover pan and bake 35 minutes. Turn and baste chicken twice.
Remove picks, place each chicken roll on an orange slice on heated platter; spoon sauce over and garnish with peel and parsley. Serves 6.

--Pat Maddox

"A well-made sauce will make even an elephant
Or a grandfather palatable." Frimod de La Reyniere

SAUCE FOR HAM: Combine 1 cup Port, ½ cup raisins, ½ cup grated orange peel, and ¼ tsp. salt in a saucepan over low heat. When hot stir in 1½ tsps. cornstarch mixed with ½ cup water; stir until thickened and serve over sliced ham.

BROCCOLI CASSEROLE

2 pkgs. frozen broccoli spears
1 can mushroom soup
1 cup mayonnaise
1 medium onion, chopped
1 cup pecans (optional)

2 eggs, well beaten
1 cup sharp cheese, grated
2 cups buttered bread crumbs
Salt to taste

Cook broccoli as directed and cut in 1-inch pieces. Add onions, mayonnaise, nuts and one-half of the cheese. Add the eggs, mix and put in a 1½-quart casserole. Sprinkle with remaining cheese, and bread crumbs. Bake at 350 degrees for 30 minutes or until heated through. Serves 6 to 8.

--*Birthe Wiik*
Scandinavian Lodge

PECAN CRUNCH

3 eggs
½ tsp. baking powder
1 cup sugar
11 graham crackers

1 cup chopped pecans
1 tsp. vanilla
Whipped cream

Beat eggs and baking powder; add sugar slowly and beat until thickened. Crush graham crackers and add to egg mixture. Add pecans and vanilla and blend well. Pour into a buttered 10-inch glass pie plate. Bake at 350 degrees for 30 minutes. Serve with whipped cream.

--*Jean Consalus*

Fourth Of July Rodeo

James Crawford, the founder of Steamboat Springs, sponsored the first Fourth of July celebration in 1876. It was mainly a flag raising ceremony and picnic which was attended by the settlers and Indians in the area. Over the years the event has grown into a major celebration which everyone looks forward to. Now there is a parade down Lincoln Avenue, a dance, fireworks and the all important rodeo.

The area has long been headquarters for the region's cattle industry and cowboys from near and far come to compete in the rodeo. The first bucking events were added in 1904 and the first permanent arena was built in Brooklyn in 1927. There it has remained...the site of a rootin' tootin', bone bustin' celebration in the summer sun.

Everyone picnics on July 4th. It seems as much a part of our heritage as flag waving and "The Star Spangled Banner." Picnics though have acquired an air of sophistication over the years. Why not make your next one a little different? Take a chafing dish along to keep these meatballs hot for nibbling with cocktails or beer.

CHAFING DISH MEATBALLS AND FRANKS

2 lbs. ground chuck	1 large grated onion
1 egg, beaten	Salt and pepper to taste

Combine and shape into 50 to 60 small meatballs. No need to brown them...just drop into a mixture of:

1 bottle chili sauce	Juice of 1 lemon
1 cup grape jelly	

Simmer until meatballs are done. Add:

2 lbs. frankfurters, sliced on the diagonal ½-inch thick

Cook until heated through. (Can be frozen at this point; defrost and reheat slowly.) Serve with cocktail picks from your chafing dish. Serves 8.

—*Carol Mitchell*

74

BARBECUED ITALIAN SAUSAGES

Sauce:

1/3 cup vinegar
1/3 cup water
3 Tbs. brown sugar
1 Tbs. Dijon style mustard
½ tsp. pepper
2 tsps. salt

¼ tsp. cayenne pepper
½ lemon, seeded
1 medium onion, chopped
1/3 cup butter
2/3 cup catsup
3 Tbs. Worcestershire Sauce

Combine all ingredients in a saucepan except catsup and
Worcestershire Sauce. Simmer for 20 minutes. Add remaining
ingredients and bring to a boil. Remove from heat and press
the lemon against side of pan to remove juices; discard.
Stir well. Makes 2 cups of sauce. Use on chicken or ribs
also.

Grill Italian sausages over low coals, basting often with the
barbecue sauce. Cook until browned allowing at least one
per person.

--Pat Maddox

PARMESAN GRILLED POTATOES

Bake potatoes until firm, not soft. Peel and slice in ½-inch
slices. Wrap in foil. Combine 1 stick softened butter, 1
Tbs. Parmesan cheese, 1½ tsps. each basil and marjoram, salt
and pepper to taste. Beat until fluffy and pack in covered
container. Just before serving, heat potatoes on grill then
top with butter. Makes ½ cup.

SAUERKRAUT SALAD

1 large jar sauerkraut
1 cup sugar
1 cup chopped green pepper

1 cup chopped onion
Pimiento, if desired

Mix well; cover and refrigerate at least 24 hours. Use less
sugar if recipe is doubled. Serves 8 to 10.

--Cookbook Committee

MANDARIN CAKE

1 cup sugar
1 cup flour
1 egg
1 tsp. soda
1 tsp. vanilla

¼ tsp. salt
½ cup chopped nuts
Small can Mandarin oranges,
    drained

Combine all ingredients and beat for 3 minutes on medium speed
of mixer. Pour into a lightly greased 8 x 8-inch pan. Bake
35 minutes at 350 degrees.

Topping:

3/4 cup brown sugar
3 tsps. milk

1 Tbs. butter

Bring to a boil and pour over cake as soon as you remove it
from the oven. Store in refrigerator until ready to serve.

--Mindy Williams

 ## BOLOGNA SALAD

12 ozs. chunk bologna, cubed
4 large potatoes, cooked,
    peeled and cubed
1 apple, cored and cubed
½ cup pickled beets, cut in
    strips
¼ cup dill pickle, chopped

1 small onion, chopped
1 cup sour cream
2 Tbs. Dijon mustard
2 Tbs. pickled beet juice
¼ tsp. salt
¼ tsp. ground allspice

Combine the first six ingredients in a mixing bowl. Combine
the remaining ingredients and
fold into the bologna mixture.
Chill at least 2 hours before
serving. Serves 6.

A Rancher

TUNA TREASURE

1 7-oz. can tuna, drained
1 8-oz. jar artichokes,
  drained
2 Tbs. flour
3 Tbs. butter
1½ cups milk

½ tsp. salt
Black pepper to taste
1 Tbs. Worcestershire sauce
1 4-oz. can sliced mushrooms,
  drained
¼ cup grated Parmesan cheese

Arrange artichokes in a buttered 1-quart casserole dish; top
with tuna. Add flour to butter in a saucepan and slowly add
milk. Cook over medium heat until thickened; season and add
the mushrooms. Pour sauce over the tuna mixture; sprinkle
with cheese. Bake 20 minutes at 375 degrees. Serves 4.

NOTE: For a marvelous luncheon dish substitute shrimp for
     tuna, sherry for Worcestershire sauce and add 1 Tbs.
     soy sauce. Entirely different taste treat!

GINGER NUT SCONES

Good for breakfast with honey or jam and a marvelous accompaniment for salads or casseroles at lunch.

2 cups flour
1 tsp. baking powder
½ tsp. salt
½ cup butter or margarine,
  softened
2/3 cup sugar
¼ cup crystallized ginger,
  chopped

¼ cup toasted pecans or
  walnuts, chopped
1 egg, beaten
3/4 cup milk
1 egg, beaten
Sugar and cinnamon

Sift flour, baking powder and salt together; cut in butter
or margarine. Add sugar, ginger and walnuts with 1 egg and
milk; stir to make a soft dough. Turn dough out onto a
lightly floured pastry board; roll into an 8-inch circle.
Place dough circle onto a lightly greased cookie sheet and
cut into 8 wedges. Brush with second egg and sprinkle with
mixture of cinnamon and sugar. Bake at 425 degrees for 15
minutes or until golden brown. Serve warm. Makes 8 scones.

Can you visualize a strawberry too large to fit into a water glass? That's what the oldtimers claimed about berries grown in a lush meadowland north of Steamboat Springs. The berries were called Remington after a Kansas farmer who settled in the area to raise strawberries. Uniquely, because of the 7000-foot-plus elevation, the berries ripened long after plants at lower elevations thus creating an instant market.

The Routt County Strawberry Company was formed in 1910 and the first 528 crates were shipped to markets in 1911. Farmers turned their acres into strawberry-producing fields, a Strawberry Festival was inaugurated to celebrate the harvest, and land prices in the area soared. But the strawberry boom ended when mother nature dealt it an icy blow. Early frosts ruined crops in 1915 and 1916...raising strawberries in the mountains then, as now, was a risky business.

Strawberry Park now houses elegant ranch homes with area hostesses serving strawberries...not from water glasses but from crystal bowls.

STRAWBERRY SOUP

1½ cups water
3/4 cup rose' wine (or red wine)
½ cup sugar
2 Tbs. fresh lemon juice
1 stick cinnamon

½ tsp. whole allspice (tie in cheesecloth)
1 quart fresh strawberries, stemmed and pureed
½ cup whipping cream
¼ to ½ cup sour cream

Combine water, wine, sugar, lemon juice, cinnamon and all-spice. Boil, uncovered, 15 minutes, stirring occasionally. Add strawberry puree and boil, stirring, 10 minutes longer. Discard cinnamon and allspice; cool.
Whip cream and combine with sour cream. Fold into strawberry mixture and refrigerate. Let stand at room temperature for 15 minutes before serving. Makes 1½ quarts.

STRAWBERRY BREAD

3 cups sifted flour
1 tsp. soda
1 tsp. salt
2 cups sugar
4 eggs, beaten

2 cups strawberries
1 Tbs. cinnamon
1¼ cups vegetable oil
1¼ cups chopped pecans

Sift dry ingredients together and set aside. Mix eggs, oil, nuts and strawberries together and add to dry ingredients, stirring just enough to moisten. Pour into 2 greased, standard-size loaf pans. Bake for 1 hour at 350 degrees. Let loaves cool 5 minutes before removing from pans. Cool on wire racks.

--*Tina Richie*
Arlington, Texas

CHOCOLATE AMARETTO FONDUE WITH STRAWBERRIES

2½ lbs. Hershey's chocolate
1½ sticks butter

1 cup half and half
½ cup Amaretto

Combine mixtures and heat in fondue or crock pot, slowly, until chocolate melts. Serve with strawberries or a tray of bite-size assorted fruits for dipping.

--*Marilyn McCaulley*

AVACADO CITRUS SALAD

Peel and chop into bite-size pieces, 1 avacado and 2 oranges. Slice ½-pint strawberries in half. Toss with as much coconut as your taste demands and add a little honey for sweetness. Sprinkle with chopped walnuts to serve. Serves 4.

--*Russ Drobney*
Las Vegas, Nevada

MOCK STRAWBERRY MOUSSE:

In your blender whip together 1 package of frozen strawberries (or raspberries or peaches) with 1 cup of sugar, 1 tablespoon vanilla, and 1 pint sour cream. Refreeze. Serves 4.

"This has been a favorite of my children for 25 years."
--*Regina Hollberg*

STRAWBERRIES ROMANOFF

1 quart vanilla ice cream
1 pint whipping cream, whipped
1 Tbs. lemon juice
½ cup Cointreau

¼ cup rum
1 pint strawberries
Sugar

Whip ice cream slightly and fold in whipped cream; add lemon
juice and liqueurs. Freeze in a plastic container. When
ready to serve, let soften slightly and spoon onto chilled
plates. Combine strawberries and sugar to taste and heap
berries over creamed mixture. If using frozen berries,
drain well and do not add sugar. Serves 6 to 8.

STRAWBERRY 7-UP PIE: Cook 1 cup sugar, 3 Tbs. cornstarch,
1 small bottle 7-Up, and a few drops
of red food coloring until thick. Cool. Add 1 pint fresh
strawberries, sliced and pour mixture into a 9-inch baked
pie shell. When ready to serve, top with 1 cup heavy cream,
whipped. Garnish with whole berries.

STRAWBERRY BUTTER: One pint fresh strawberries, or 10 ounces
frozen, drained, ½ lb. unsalted butter, 1
cup powdered sugar; if using frozen berries use ½ cup. Put
ingredients in blender in order given. Blend until smooth
and creamy. If mixture appears to curdle, don't despair, continue blending until creamy. Chill. Serve with toast, strawberry bread, biscuits or waffles. Makes 2½ cups.

And for strawberries from your freezer...

STRAWBERRIES AND HAM SUPREME

1 ham slice, cut 1-inch thick
½ tsp. dry mustard

1 10-oz. pkg. frozen strawberries, thawed
6 whole cloves

Slash around edge of ham and spread mustard over it. Pierce
with cloves. Drain the thawed strawberries and pour juice
over ham. Bake at 350 degrees for 45 minutes. Scatter remaining berries over ham and bake 15 minutes longer. Serves 4.

"A show-stopping company casserole"

CHICKEN ALMONDZINI

3/4 cup mayonnaise
1/3 cup flour
2 Tbs. instant minced onion
1 tsp. garlic salt
2¼ cups milk
1 cup Swiss cheese, grated
1/3 cup dry white wine
7 ozs. spaghetti, cooked
  and drained

2 cups chopped cooked chicken
  or turkey
1 10-oz. pkg. frozen chopped
  broccoli, thawed and drained
1¼ cups sliced almonds
1 4-oz. can sliced mushrooms,
  drained
¼ cup chopped pimiento
Parmesan cheese

In a medium saucepan, combine mayonnaise, flour and seasonings. Gradually add milk; cook over low heat, stirring constantly, until thickened. Add cheese and wine; stir until the cheese melts. Combine mayonnaise mixture, spaghetti, chicken, broccoli, mushrooms, pimiento and 3/4 cup chopped almonds; toss lightly. Pour into a buttered 11 x 7-inch baking dish and top with remaining almonds. Bake at 350 degrees for 40 to 45 minutes or until heated through. Serve with grated Parmesan cheese. Serves 6 to 8. *--Carol Mitchell*

SCALLOPED CORN AND OYSTERS

1 1-lb. can (2 cups) cream-
  style corn
1 can frozen condensed
  oyster stew, thawed
1 cup medium cracker crumbs
  (20-22 crackers)

1 cup milk
¼ cup finely chopped celery
1 slightly beaten egg
1 Tbs. finely chopped pimiento
¼ tsp. salt
Dash pepper

Topping: 2 Tbs. butter, melted
         ½ cup medium cracker crumbs (10-11 crackers)

Combine corn, oyster stew, 1 cup cracker crumbs, milk, celery, egg, pimiento, salt and pepper. Pour into greased 1½-quart casserole. Combine butter and ½ cup cracker crumbs; sprinkle over corn mixture in wreath design. Bake at 350 degrees for 60 minutes until knife inserted halfway between center and edge comes out clean. Makes 6 servings.

--Mae Bryant

81

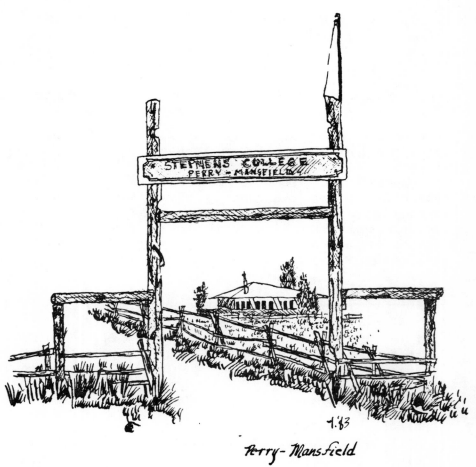

Perry-Mansfield

They had a dream...a dream of dancing in the mountains. So
it was that in 1914 Marjorie Perry and Portia Mansfield,
newly won degrees from Smith College tucked under their
arms, arrived in the Rocky Mountains to launch the Perry-
Mansfield Dance Camp in Strawberry Park. Later they would
dance and teach such notables as Martha Graham, Lee Remick,
Dustin Hoffman, and Julie Harris. And they taught them to
appreciate the mountains, animals, forests, and streams,
to exist in the wilderness, and to perform before audiences.

During the early years of the camp, horseback riding was
emphasized...not riding in a ring but into the hills and
on overnight pack trips. Sleeping under the stars and fishing for one's supper were things the people of Steamboat
could understand. Dancing though was foreign to this town
of ranchers, particularly the type performed by the students
in flimsy costumes and toe shoes. It was not until the 1940's
when the school began to produce plays and perform for the
public that it was fully supported by the town. During that
period Marjorie Perry and Portia Mansfield became legendary.

In 1965 Stephens College assumed ownership of Perry-Mansfield
and classes earned formal college credits for the students.
This has somewhat altered the original relaxed atmosphere
since a certain amount of time must be spent in organized
classes, but management has strived to keep the image of
earlier years alive. Each year during the first week of
camp a dance concert is presented. A month later the older
students perform "An Evening of Scenes." Their always en-
thusiastic audiences include residents and visitors of Routt
County who come to appreciate and long remember the legacy
of two girls from Smith College who had a dream...a dream
of dancing in the mountains.

*One might call a beautifully prepared dinner "An Evening of
Scenes" with the entree the star attraction. A supporting
cast of salad, spiced wine, and home baked rolls should
demand a standing ovation.*

ORANGE FLAVORED WINE

4 cups dry white or red wine
1¼ cups sugar

1/4 cup each light rum and
    grated orange rind
1 Tbs. whole cloves

Combine the mixture in a jar and stir until sugar dissolves.
Seal with a lid. Refrigerate overnight or up to 3 weeks,
shaking the jar at least once daily. Strain through a fine
sieve and serve very cold. Can be kept, corked, in dark
bottles in a cool place. Makes 5½ cups.

SPINACH BALLS

4 10-oz. pkgs. chopped
  spinach
1 8-oz. pkg. Pepperidge Farm
  stuffing mix
1/3 cup minced onions
8 eggs

1 cup Parmesan cheese, grated
1½ cups melted butter or
  margarine
1 tsp. thyme
Garlic salt to taste

Cook spinach to package directions and drain very well. Add
the remaining ingredients and form into small balls. Refrigerate overnight. Bake at 300 degrees on a lightly
greased cookie sheet for 30 minutes. Serves 12. Recipe can
be cut in half.

--Janet Way

SMOKY GALLIANO CHICKEN BREASTS

2 whole broiler-fryer chicken
  breasts halved, boned and
  skinned
1 Tbs. liquid smoke
½ tsp. salt
¼ cup flour
2 Tbs. cooking oil
1 tsp. instant chicken
  bouillon

½ cup boiling water
1 Tbs. Galliano
¼ cup plus 3 Tbs. orange
  juice
2 Tbs. minced onion
1 tsp. cornstarch
2 Tbs. chopped parsley
Cooked rice or noodles

On a hard surface with meat mallet or similar flattening
utensil, pound chicken to ¼-inch thickness. Brush chicken
with liquid smoke, then sprinkle it with salt. Place flour

in a shallow dish. Add chicken one piece at a time, dredging to coat chicken on all sides. Place oil in a medium skillet over moderate heat. Add chicken; cook over moderate heat until chicken is brown on both sides, about 7 minutes. In a small bowl, dissolve bouillon in water. Add Galliano and 3 tablespoons of the orange juice. Mix well. Add bouillon mixture and onion to chicken in skillet. Simmer covered over low heat about 15 minutes or until chicken is fork tender. Remove chicken to serving platter. In a small bowl, mix together until smooth cornstarch and remaining ¼-cup orange juice; stir into skillet with parsley. Cook over moderate heat, stirring constantly, until thickened. Spoon sauce over chicken. Serve with rice or noodles. Serves 4.

--Jan Vail

For a different entree, you might consider popping this in the oven to bake while you are enjoying the shows.

SATURDAY NITE CHICKEN

Cut one 3-1b. chicken into serving pieces and put in a baking dish you can serve from. Sprinkle with garlic salt, paprika, and pepper. Combine 1 cup whipping cream and 1 can cream of mushroom soup; pour over chicken. Bake at 325 degrees for 2 hours. Serves 4.

--Heidi Bowes

APRICOT ORANGE SALAD

12 ozs. apricot nectar
1 large size lemon Jello
1 3-oz. pkg. cream cheese

1 cup whipping cream
1 can Mandarin oranges

Heat nectar to boiling; add Jello. Stir to dissolve and cool. Mix some of the Jello mixture with cream cheese and whip until smooth. Whip cream until stiff peaks form; fold into cream cheese and stir in the nectar mixture. Stir in oranges and chill in a pretty mold. Serves 6 to 8.

--Diane Franklin

FUDGE SUNDAE PIE

1 cup evaporated milk
1 6-oz. pkg. semi-sweet
  chocolate morsels
1 cup miniature marshmallows

¼ tsp. salt
Vanilla Wafers
1 pint vanilla ice cream
Pecan halves

Combine milk, chocolate morsels, marshmallows and salt in a
saucepan and stir over medium heat until melted and mixture
thickens. Cool to room temperature. Line a 9-inch pie
plate with vanilla wafers; cover with half the ice cream.
Spoon over half the chocolate mixture. Repeat layers.
Garnish with pecan halves. Freeze until firm (3 to 5
hours). Serves 6 to 8.

--Helen Reynolds

EASY YEAST ROLLS OR BREAD

2 pkgs. dry yeast
2 cups warm water
½ cup sugar
1 egg

2 tsp. salt
6½ to 7 cups white unbleached
  flour
¼ cup melted margarine

Dissolve yeast in warm water, add sugar, salt and egg. Mix.
Add 3½ cups of the flour. Mix well. Add remaining flour.
Mix. Let rise covered with a damp cloth for about 2 hours
or in the refrigerator overnight.

Two hours before baking, form into rolls (clover or Parker)
or into 3 braided loaves of bread. Brush with egg white
and sprinkle with poppy seeds or sesame seeds. Cover with
a damp cloth and let rise for about 2 hours or until double
in size. Bake at 425 degrees for 10 minutes for rolls, 400
degrees for 20 minutes for bread. Makes 3 dozen rolls or 3
loaves bread.

--Diane Franklin

 PEACHY SHRIMP: Peel, halve and pit large fresh peaches. Combine chilled cooked shrimp, chopped celery,
minced green onion, and enough cocktail sauce
to moisten. Mound into center of each half.
Top with toasted almonds. Substitute chicken
or ham and combine with chutney and mayonnaise.

Fish Creek Falls

"Every stream in our valley forces its way through some gorge or down some rugged canyon. The most beautiful of these watery ways is Fish Creek Falls, three miles west of Steamboat Springs on a creek of the same name..."

PILOT - 1892

With a drop of more than 260 feet, Fish Creek Falls is a spectacular waterfall easily accessible by automobile with only a short walk to the falls. It has been a popular gathering place for picnics for as long as there have been people in the valley. The roar of the falls in early spring, and the color of aspen in the fall attract visitors and residents to the area until snow blocks their way and even then cross country skiers make their way to a wintry wonderland of icicles and snow-draped trees.

Through the years the falls had been privately owned with public access only by informal agreement with the various owners. Eventually, Bob Adams, former Energy Fuels owner, completed a land trade that made Fish Creek Falls part of the Routt National Forest. Through his generosity, one of Northwest Colorado's most beautiful natural features will rest forever in the public domain.

You will find picnic tables available for your convenience at this picturesque spot so plan to spend several hours hiking to the top of the falls and enjoying a lunch or early supper...

CHEDDAR BURGERS

1½ lbs. ground beef	1 tsp. salt
2 cups grated sharp Cheddar	1 tsp. smoked salt
1 Tbs. chili sauce	½ tsp. cracked pepper
¼ cup minced onion	

Combine all ingredients; mix lightly. Shape into six patties and grill to desired doneness. Serve on warm buttered buns.

FROZEN SLAW

1 medium head cabbage
1 Tbs. salt
3 stalks celery, finely
  chopped
3 red or green bell peppers,
  chopped

1 cup white vinegar
2 cups granulated sugar
½ cup water
1 tsp. mustard seed
1 tsp. celery seed

Finely chop the cabbage and add the salt. Mix and let stand for one hour. Squeeze out any accumulated liquid. Add the celery and green peppers.
Combine the remaining ingredients in a saucepan and bring to a boil. Boil one minute and pour over the cabbage mixture. Chill well before serving. This will keep in the refrigerator for three weeks or may be frozen. If not used at one time, it can even be refrozen! Serves 8.

--Doris Scott

CALICO BEANS

1 can pork and beans
1 can kidney beans
1 can butter beans

½ lb. hamburger
½ lb. bacon
½ cup sliced hot dogs

Combine beans in a large bean pot. In a large skillet fry hamburger, bacon and hot dogs together; drain fat from pan and add meats to beans.

Sauce:

½ cup catsup
½ cup sugar
½ cup brown sugar

2 Tbs. mustard
½ tsp. salt
1 large onion, diced

Combine all the ingredients and pour over bean mixture. Bake at 350 degrees for one hour. Best if made a day ahead. Reheat to serve. Serves 8 to 10.

--Doris Scott

And for those of you who do not care for the usual thick and calorie-laden hamburger, this recipe was concocted to answer your demands...

DEVILED HAMBURGERS

1 lb. very lean ground beef round
1/3 cup chili sauce
1½ tsps. Dijon mustard
1½ tsps. grated horseradish
1 small onion, minced

1½ tsps. Worcestershire or steak sauce
1 tsp. salt
Generous dash of pepper
6 sandwich type hamburger buns or English muffins

Halve the buns or muffins and toast under the broiler. Lightly combine the remaining ingredients. Spread the meat mixture in a thin layer over both top and bottom toasted sides; meat should overlap the bun slightly. Broil about 5 inches from heat for 7 to 10 minutes or until meat is cooked to your taste. Serve immediately.

VARIATIONS: During the last 2 minutes of broiling, top bottom half with Cheddar, Swiss or bleu cheese. Serve with tomato slices and/or thinly sliced avocado. Onion? By all means!

MOLDED PINEAPPLE SALAD

1 pkg. lime or lemon gelatin
1 cup boiling water
1 can crushed pineapple
1 3-oz. pkg. cream cheese

1/3 cup chopped celery
½ cup chopped nuts
1 cup whipping cream

Add boiling water to gelatin and dissolve. Drain pineapple and add enough water to make 3/4 cup and add to gelatin. Chill until partially set. Combine cream cheese, pineapple, celery and nuts. Mix until creamy; add to gelatin mixture. Whip the cream to stiff peaks and fold into the pineapple mixture. Pour into a mold and chill until set. Serves 8.

--*Florence Price*

Nothing tastes quite as good on a picnic as homemade ice cream and cookies. When both are easy to make so much the better!

ICE CREAM

4 eggs
2 cans sweetened condensed
  milk
1 quart whipping cream

1½ Tbs. vanilla (or other
   flavorings as desired)
1½ quarts milk (approximately)

Beat eggs, add condensed milk and mix well. Add cream, flavorings, and enough milk to fill freezer can to manufacturer's directions. Freeze and pack to take to picnic site.

--*Susan Hoffner*

EASY PEANUT BUTTER COOKIES

1 cup peanut butter
1 cup sugar

1 large egg

Combine and roll into small balls; press with a fork to flatten. Bake at 350 degrees for 8 minutes. Makes 2 dozen.

--*Carolyn Williams*

If you prefer to visit the falls and return home for dinner, this beef brisket can be cooking while you enjoy the scenery...

SMOKY BEEF BRISKET

6 lbs. beef brisket, trimmed
  of fat
2 Tbs. liquid smoke

1 Tbs. garlic salt
2 Tbs. celery salt
2 Tbs. Worcestershire Sauce

Rub the beef brisket with liquid smoke, garlic and celery salt. Wrap in foil and refrigerate overnight. On the next day rub with 2 more tablespoons liquid smoke and 2 tablespoons Worcestershire sauce. Salt to taste and wrap in an airtight foil package. Bake at 300 degrees for six hours... longer will not hurt. Serves 6 to 8.

--*Malvina Carothers*

Mountain Golfing

Picture a lonely shepherd strolling along a Scottish moor tending elusive sheep with a crooked stick. Bored with heather, the ever constant wind, and the bleatings of his wooly companions, he takes his crook, aims a small stone at a rabbit hole and makes the first hole-in-one in history. Some say the Romans invented the game of golf, the French lay claim to inventing almost everything, but golf is Scottish in the eyes of most who follow the sport. And golfing at Steamboat is a never-to-be forgotten experience.

The first day of each season members of the Ladies Golf Association will be found at the Municipal Course or at the Club Course operated by the Sheraton at Steamboat. They will spend many sunny days in devilish pursuit of that little white ball until the first snow flies.

History reveals that Mary Queen of Scots knocked around a few golf balls in her day, and with all the servants at her disposal in the castle, preparation of dinner was of no concern. So ladies, as your ball travels along (or in) the rushing waters of Fish Creek and you have just swung the 99th time, your thoughts probably turn to the 19th hole...and eventually to the fact that company is coming for dinner. Unlike Mary, there are no servants in your castle so a dish prepared ahead of time assures a worry-free day of golfing in the mountains.

CHICKEN TETRAZZINI

1 chicken	1 cup frozen peas
3/4 tsp. onion salt	2 Tbs. flour
3/4 tsp. celery salt	½ tsp. paprika
½ lb. spaghetti	1/8 tsp. nutmeg
6 Tbs. butter	2½ cups reserved chicken broth
½ lb. mushrooms	1 cup heavy cream
1 Tbs. lemon juice	¼ cup sherry
¼ cup toasted slivered almonds	Grated Parmesan cheese

Cook chicken in salted water (bay leaf and onion may be added for flavor) until tender. Remove skin and bones, leaving

pieces rather large. Reserve 2½ cups of cooking broth. To
the rest of the broth add 3 cups water and 2 tsp. salt. Bring
to a boil. Add the spaghetti and cook about 6 minutes, stirring occasionally. (Spaghetti should be al dente - do not
overcook.) Drain well. Meanwhile (or beforehand) melt 3 Tbs.
of the butter, add mushrooms (sliced), ½ tsp. salt and the
lemon juice. Cook until mushrooms are lightly browned. Mix
with the spaghetti. In a sauce pan melt the remaining butter.
Add the flour, onion and celery salt, paprika, nutmeg, and
cook for 1 minute, stirring constantly. Add sherry and cook
a moment longer, then add chicken broth and cook until
slightly thickened (sauce will be thin). Add the chicken and
the cream. Mix the sauce with the spaghetti, add the peas
and almonds. Place mixture in a shallow casserole and cover
with the Parmesan cheese. Refrigerate until the next day.
Preheat oven to 375 degrees. Cook until hot, bubbly and
lightly browned (approximately ½ hour).

--Marian Tolles

*Or, if you happen to have some left-over chicken or turkey,
you might substitute this easy-to-prepare casserole...*

TURKEY CHEESE CASSEROLE

Make a white sauce:

¼ cup butter	1½ tsps. salt
4 Tbs. flour	Pepper to taste
2 cups milk	

Melt butter, stir in flour and cook until smooth. Gradually
add milk and stir until thickened; add seasoning. Combine
with the following ingredients:

2 cups turkey, diced	½ cup mushrooms (fresh or
1½ cups cooked rice	canned)
3/4 cup cheese, grated	¼ cup pimiento, chopped
	3/4 cup chopped nuts

Place in a buttered 2-quart baking dish. Sprinkle with 3/4
cup buttered bread crumbs. Bake at 325 degrees for about 25
minutes or until bubbly and brown. Serves 6 to 8.

--Ruth Valdeck

A welcomed accompaniment to any casserole dish...

WATERMELON PICKLES

7 lbs. watermelon rinds

Cut off all pink and green peeling. Cut in small chunks, cover with water and 1 tsp. tumeric (scant measure). Cook until done but still firm. Drain for 12 hours.

Syrup:

7 cups sugar	½ tsp. oil of cloves
2 cups vinegar	½ tsp. oil of cinnamon

Combine the ingredients (oil of cloves and cinnamon can be purchased at a drug store) and bring to a boil to dissolve. Pour hot syrup over drained rind and let stand for 24 hours. Pour syrup off and heat to boiling. Pour over rind and let stand another 24 hours. Repeat.
Heat syrup and rinds together and pack into hot sterilized jars. Seal.

--Elaine Stroncek

PEAR PICKLES

4 dozen firm-ripe pears	1 piece ginger root
3 cups sugar	½ lemon, thinly sliced
1 Tbs. mixed pickling spices	2½ cups water
1 tsp. whole cloves	1½ cups vinegar

Pare and core pears. Tie spices in a cheesecloth bag; add to remaining gredients; simmer 5 minutes. Add pears, a layer at a time, and cook gently until just tender, about 15 minutes. Carefully remove pears. Repeat until all pears are cooked. Pour boiling syrup over pears. Pack pears into hot jars, leaving ¼-inch head space. Remove spice bag. Heat syrup to boiling. Pour boiling syrup over pears, leaving ¼-inch head space. Remove air bubbles. Adjust caps. Process pints and quarts 15 minutes in boiling water bath. Yield: 3 to 4 pints.

--Mae Bryant

QUICK CHERRY SALAD

Dissolve 1 small box cherry flavored Jello in 1 cup boiling water. Add 1 can cherry pie filling and 1 cup grated apples. Chill until firm in an 8-inch square dish. Cut in squares to serve.

NOTE: Chopped nuts, whipped cream, or a cream cheese frosting may be added but they are just "calorie extras" as the salad is delicious "as is."

--Maxine Elliott

MOM'S MINT BROWNIES

1 cup sugar
½ cup margarine
4 eggs
1 cup flour
½ tsp. salt

1 16-oz. can Hershey's
  Chocolate Syrup
1 tsp. vanilla
½ cup chopped nuts

Cream sugar and margarine; add eggs one at a time. Add flour, salt, syrup and vanilla; stir in nuts. Bake at 350 degrees for 30 minutes in a greased 13 x 9-inch pan. Cool.

Second Layer:

2 cups powdered sugar
½ cup margarine

2 Tbs. creme de menthe

Blend and spread over cooled brownie mixture.

Third Layer:

1 cup chocolate chips

6 Tbs. margarine

Melt and cool slightly. Spread over second layer. Cut in squares to serve.

--Marilyn McCaulley

HAPPY TEA: Combine 1 cup strong, freshly brewed tea, 1 cup white port or any dessert wine, and 2 tablespoons lemon juice. Serve over ice in tall glasses; garnish with orange slices. Serves 2 generously.

The Sleeping Giant

Guarding the town to the west is Steamboat's very own Sleeping Giant Mountain. His outline is easily discernible when he covers himself with a blanket of snow for his winter nap. Come spring he sheds his covering to reveal his bedtime companions...rattlesnakes! Oddly, this is the only place in Routt County where they may be found. Because of their presence, the Giant is sometimes called Rattlesnake Mountain.

Rattlesnakes might make charming companions for the Giant, and in Oriental countries they are considered a culinary delicacy. But for most, a more popular entree would be a combination of sausage and cheese or sausage and rice.

SAUSAGE AND RICE CASSEROLE

1 lb. sausage (pork, elk or venison)
1 onion, chopped
2 stalks celery, chopped
2 envelopes noodle soup mix (small)

1 can cream of chicken soup
2 cans water
Soy sauce to taste
1½ cups Minute Rice

Brown the sausage, onion and celery; drain off fat. Add remaining ingredients except rice and simmer for 5 minutes. Add rice and remove from heat and let stand until rice is tender. Serve from the pan or turn into a casserole dish and heat a few minutes in the oven. Serves 4 to 6.

--Joyce Taylor

ITALIAN SAUSAGE QUICHE

3/4 lb. Italian sausage
2/3 cup ricotta cheese
¼ cup green pepper, chopped
1 4-oz. can mushrooms, drained

3 Tbs. parsley, chopped
1/3 cup Parmesan cheese, grated
¼ tsp. salt

Brown sausage, green pepper, and mushrooms; drain off excess fat. Add remaining ingredients and set aside.

95

Custard:

4 eggs
3/4 cup milk
3/4 cup evaporated milk
2 Tbs. melted butter

1 Tbs. flour
Pinch of each, salt, cayenne,
  and nutmeg

Combine all ingredients and beat together. Add to mixture
and pour into an unbaked 9-inch pie shell.

Pie Shell:

1¼ cups flour
¼ tsp. salt
½ cup Parmesan cheese, grated

4 Tbs. butter
4 to 5 Tbs. cold water

Combine ingredients and roll on a lightly floured board. Fit
into a 9-inch pie plate. Fill with sausage mixture. Bake
at 375 degrees for 40 minutes or until center is set. Serves
4 to 6.

SAUSAGE AND CHEESE SKILLET (Italian Chili)

1 lb. Italian sausage
½ tsp. Italian seasonings
1 cup chopped onion
½ cup green pepper, chopped
1 clove garlic, minced
1 16-oz. can stewed tomatoes

1 cup tomato juice
1 4-oz. can button mushrooms
2 tsps. instant beef bouillon
  (or 2 cubes)
1 cup Parmesan and Romano
  cheese
Corn chips

Brown meat in a large skillet; drain off fat. Add onion,
pepper and garlic; stir fry until tender. Add tomato juice,
mushrooms, bouillon and seasonings. Simmer uncovered about
30 minutes. Stir in ½ cup cheese, heat through and serve
over corn chips. Sprinkle with remaining cheese. Serves 4.

NOTE: You may use half ground beef and half Italian sausage
      if preferred.

--Lorna Brown

Father Francis Ciaptacz, a native of Poland and former skiing companion of Pope John Paul II, became pastor of Holy Name Catholic Church in Steamboat Springs on May 2, 1979. He said of his new town, "Oh, this is like a dream come true, the answer to a prayer I made many years ago. The mountains are so beautiful, and the skiing is just great!" He said Mass for skiers and other visitors each Sunday evening at the mountain and became a beloved friend to all who knew him. Often he expressed the desire to establish an inter-faith chapel, "some clear symbol of God at the ski area."

Father Francis died in his sleep on June 7, 1982 and was buried in the Steamboat cemetery. As one stands near his gravesite, Sleeping Giant Mountain forms a fitting backdrop for this giant of a man. His niece, Irene Ciaptacz of Denver, tells us this was one of his favorite soups...

POLISH KUPNIK

1 lb. pork (preferably lean pork chops)
1 cup barley
2 medium carrots, chopped
1 medium onion, chopped
1 medium turnip, chopped
Fresh dill or parsley
Salt and pepper to taste

Cover meat with cold water and bring to a boil; clean off meat "scum" as it collects. Cook for 30 minutes. Add barley and simmer for 30 minutes. Remove meat from pot, cool and debone. Return to pot with the carrots, onion and turnip; simmer another 30 minutes or until barley and vegetables are cooked. Garnish with fresh dill or parsley. If soup becomes too thick, add more water. Serves 4 to 6.

NOTE: Irene adds the white root of parsley, chopped, after the first 30 minutes of cooking. This is a pleasant addition but not always easily found.

--Irene Ciaptacz

CHERRY DELIGHT:
Combine 1 large carton Cool Whip, 1 can sweetened condensed milk, 1 can cherry pie filling, 1 small can crushed pineapple, drained, and ½ cup chopped nuts. Chill. Serves 8.

--Carolyn Williams

Soups and stews take on a new dimension when accompanied by an interesting side dish...

ONION SHORTCAKE

1 large onion, thinly sliced	Generous dash cayenne pepper
¼ cup butter	1 cup sour cream
1½ cups corn muffin mix	¼ tsp. salt
1 egg, beaten	¼ tsp. dill weed
1/3 cup milk	1 cup sharp Cheddar cheese,
1 cup cream-style corn	grated

Saute onion in butter until transparent. Combine muffin mix, egg, milk, corn and cayenne. Place in a buttered 8-inch square pan. Add sour cream, salt, dill weed and ½ cup cheese to the onions and spread over the muffin batter. Sprinkle with remaining cheese. Bake at 425 degrees 25 to 30 minutes. Cut in squares and serve warm. Makes 9 servings.

COLORADO APPLESAUCE CAKE

2 cups sifted flour	½ cup shortening
1½ cups sugar	1½ cups unsweetened applesauce
1½ tsps. soda	2 eggs, beaten
1 tsp. salt	3/4 cup chopped raisins
2 Tbs. cocoa	3/4 cup chopped dates
½ tsp. each cinnamon, cloves,	3/4 cup chopped nuts
nutmeg, and allspice	

Topping: ½ cup chopped nuts plus 2 Tbs. sugar

Sift flour, sugar, soda, cocoa, and spices into mixing bowl. Drop in shortening, and about 2/3 of the applesauce. Beat 150 strokes, scraping bowl and spoon often. Add eggs and beat 250 strokes. Add remaining applesauce and beat 50 strokes. Fold in dates, raisins and nuts; mix and pour batter into a greased and floured tube pan. Sprinkle topping over batter. Bake at 350 degrees for 1 hour and 25 to 35 minutes. The addition of candied fruit peel and/or cherries makes this a good holiday fruit cake.

--*Lillian* Hagan

Walton Creek

A search for rabbits up near the "Ears" might leave one empty handed. If so, an otherwise beautiful day can be salvaged by trying one's luck at finding the lost gold mine on Walton Creek. The creek meanders through Meadows Campground just north of which may be found the lovely Walton Creek Falls. Legend has it that one of Colorado's best known prospectors, George A. Jackson, discovered gold along upper Walton Creek but was driven out by Indians. Over the years treasure seekers have searched for the mine, but its whereabouts remain a mystery.

Treasure hunts have long been a favorite party theme for the young. Provide them a treasure chest of snacks, hearty food, and a spirited map...and you have the makings of a guaranteed good time for children.

CHOCOLATE PEPPERMINT SHAKES

For the young treasure seekers...

1 quart milk	¼ tsp. oil of peppermint
3/4 cup chocolate syrup	Chocolate ice cream
¼ cup whipping cream	5 peppermint candy canes

Combine milk, chocolate syrup and cream in a shaker; shake to blend well. Add oil of peppermint; shake and pour into 5 tall glasses. Top each with a scoop of chocolate ice cream. Add 1 candy cane as a decorative stirrer. Serves 5.

SHRIMP DIP

2 small cans shrimp	1 tsp. cayenne pepper
2 8-oz. pkgs. cream cheese	1 small onion, grated
1 cup mayonnaise	Salt and lemon juice to taste
1 Tbs. catsup	

Soften cheese in a large mixer bowl. Add remaining ingredients. Mix at low speed until well blended. Cover and refrigerate 2 to 3 hours. Serve with crackers or dip chips. Makes 2 cups.

--Helen Reynolds

SPAGHETTI PIE

6 ozs. spaghetti
2 Tbs. butter or margarine
1/3 cup Parmesan cheese, grated
2 well beaten eggs
1 cup cottage cheese
1 lb. ground beef
1 small onion, chopped
¼ cup green pepper, chopped
1 cup tomatoes, diced
1 6-oz. can tomato paste
1 tsp. sugar
1 tsp. dried oregano
½ tsp. garlic salt
½ cup Mozzarella cheese, shredded

Cook the spaghetti to package directions; you should have about 3 cups cooked. Stir butter into hot spaghetti; add Parmesan cheese and eggs. Form spaghetti mixture into a crust in a buttered 10-inch pie pan. Spread cottage cheese over crust.
In a skillet, cook ground beef, onion, and green pepper until vegetables are tender and meat is browned; drain off excess fat. Stir in undrained tomatoes, tomato paste, sugar, oregano, and garlic salt. Turn meat mixture into crust. Bake uncovered 350 degrees for 20 minutes. Sprinkle Mozzarella cheese on top and bake 5 minutes longer. Serves 6.

--Nancy Bronennberg

You might try pork with an Oriental flavor as your entree...

PORK CHOP SUEY

1½ lbs. pork cut in 1½-inch cubes
3 Tbs. peanut oil
1 cup sliced mushrooms
1 cup sliced onions
1½ cups sliced celery
1 tsp. ginger
1 tsp. salt
1½ cups bouillon or water
4 Tbs. molasses
4 Tbs. cornstarch
3 Tbs. soy sauce
1 16-oz. can bean sprouts
Toasted slivered almonds

Cook pork and mushrooms in oil until lightly browned. Add onions, celery, seasonings and molasses. Cover and cook until meat is tender, about 30 minutes. Thicken with cornstarch mixed to a paste with a little water. Add soy sauce and bean sprouts and cook over low heat for 15 minutes. Taste to correct seasonings and serve on hot rice or fried

noodles. Sprinkle with toasted almonds just before serving.
Serves 6 to 8.   --Anne Stettner

FRESH SPINACH SALAD

1 bag fresh spinach; wash and
  tear into pieces
Fresh bean sprouts to taste
  (optional)
1 small can water chestnuts,
  drained and thinly sliced

2 hard cooked eggs, diced
4 or 5 fresh mushrooms, sliced
8 slices bacon fried crisp
  and crumbled
1 small onion, thinly sliced
  into rings

Dressing:

1 cup salad oil
½ cup wine vinegar
½ cup sugar

1/3 cup catsup
Dash of salt

Combine the ingredients and blend well. Serve over chilled
greens. Serves 6.

NOTE: Leave out the bean sprouts if serving this salad with
       the pork chop suey.
                                            --Diane Franklin

EAGLE BRAND BARS

1 cup quick cooking oatmeal
½ cup melted butter
1 cup chocolate chips
1 cup flaked coconut

1 cup chopped nuts
1 can Eagle Brand condensed
  milk

Melt butter and mix with oatmeal to form bottom layer. Spread
in a 9 x 9-inch pan. Layer the remaining ingredients (in the
order given) on top. Bake at 350 degrees for 24 to 30 minutes.
                                            --Judy L. Bagley

SOUPER POTATOES:

Top a baked potato with a hearty homemade
or canned soup like clam chowder, chili
beef, or minestrone. Add a salad...instant
lunch!

GRAHAM CRACKER COOKIES

12 double Graham crackers
1 2-oz. pkg. sliced almonds
1 cup brown sugar, packed

½ lb. melted butter or
  margarine

Use a jelly roll pan with sides. Cover bottom of pan with
crackers; sprinkle with almonds. In a saucepan, melt butter;
add sugar and cook over low heat until boiling. Boil for
4 minutes. Pour over crackers and bake at 350 degrees for
10 minutes. Cool and break into serving pieces.

--Leona Littlefield

*These delightful cookies have hidden "nuggets" of butter-
scotch inside...*

BUTTERSCOTCH PEANUT BUTTER COOKIES

1 cup butter or margarine
1 cup peanut butter
1 cup granulated sugar
1 cup brown sugar
2 eggs

2½ cups flour
1½ tsps. soda
½ tsp. salt
1 12-oz. pkg. butterscotch
  morsels

Thoroughly cream butter, peanut butter, sugars, eggs and
vanilla. Sift together dry ingredients; blend into creamed
mixture. Stir in butterscotch morsels. Shape into 1-inch
balls; roll in granulated sugar. Place 2 inches apart on
an ungreased cookie sheet. Crisscross with fork tines.
Bake at 375 degrees for 10 to 12 minutes. Cool slightly
before removing from pan. Makes 4 dozen.

--Marci Weber

 ORANGE FROSTIE: 6-oz. can frozen orange juice concentrate,
          1 cup half and half, 1 cup water, ¼ cup
sugar, 1 tsp. vanilla, 10 ice cubes. Combine in a blender
and blend until ice cubes are crushed. Serve over a scoop of
orange sherbert. Makes 5 1-cup servings.

A Hunting We Will Go

"Hunters go into paradise when they die, and
Live in this world more joyfully than any other Men."
                                   -Henry IV's master of game

Routt County was a favorite hunting ground of western Indian
tribes due to the abundance of deer, elk, buffalo, and big-
horn sheep found there. The Yampa Valley was also the nest-
ing place for wild geese, grouse, and many other species of
birds. A growing local population and severe winters, however, decreased the area wildlife drastically in the 1880's.
In 1920 stringent game regulations were implemented to pre-
serve many of the species.

In this day of modern hunting one can expect everything to
come to a screeching halt when hunting season opens.
Schools and shops close, guns are oiled, and bright orange
hats and jackets dot the mountainside. The Davey-Crockett-
for-a-day hunter climbs a mountain and hikes a trail that
he wouldn't be caught dead on any other time of the year.
He is in search of that elusive deer, elk, or game bird
that his wife secretly hopes he won't find. Oh! but your
hunter is lucky and at season's end you find yourself with
a freezer full of meat and birds. Don't despair...it's
party time. Build a safari party around your husband's
trophies, and let him brag to his heart's content as you
amaze your guests with your culinary expertise...

VENISON KABOBS

2 lbs. venison round steak	1 tsp. garlic salt
¼ cup olive oil	½ tsp. dried oregano,
¼ cup dry red wine	crumbled
2 Tbs. Worcestershire sauce	¼ tsp. pepper

Cut meat into 1-inch cubes. Mix remaining ingredients and
pour over meat in a bowl. Marinate at least 2 hours, stirring occasionally. Thread meat on skewers and broil, either
over charcoal or in the oven, until meat reaches desired
doneness, turning to brown on each side. Serves 8 to 10.
                                   --Susan O'Brien

ELK IN A PUMPKIN SHELL

Good for a fall dinner party.

4 lbs. Elk chuck steak, cut in cubes
2 Tbs. butter
4 medium onions, chopped
3 cloves garlic, pressed
2 large green peppers, chopped
1 tsp. salt
½ tsp. pepper
2 tsp. sugar

2 cans beef broth (10½ oz. each)
2 dozen dried prunes
1 pkg. dried apricots
4 yams, peeled & cut in cubes
1 bag frozen corn (1 lb. 4 oz.)
3/4 cup Madeira wine
5 Tbs. cornstarch
1 very large pumpkin (8 qt.)

Melt butter in an 8 qt. kettle, and saute meat until brown. Add onions, garlic, and green pepper and saute with meat. Mix in all other ingredients except pumpkin; cover and simmer for 1 hour. Mix cornstarch with some of the pan liquid and blend into sauce. Cut the top off the pumpkin, remove seeds and membrane and fill pumpkin with stew. Bake at 350 degrees for 1 hour. Place pumpkin on a large platter and serve from it. Serves 12.

--Susan O'Brien

Either of these vegetable dishes would be a nice accompaniment to game.

MIXED VEGETABLE CASSEROLE

1 14½-oz. can hominy, drained
1 16-oz. can stewed tomatoes, drained
1 10-oz. pkg. frozen cut okra, thawed

1½ tsps. salt
½ tsp. dried basil
6 strips bacon

Combine all ingredients except bacon in a buttered casserole dish. Arrange bacon on top. Bake, uncovered, at 350 degrees for 1 hour. Serves 6 to 8.

APPLE MINCE SQUASH

3 acorn squash
2 Tbs. butter
1 large tart apple

1 cup prepared mincemeat
  with rum
Chopped nuts
Nutmeg

Halve squash and remove seeds. Place, cut sides down, on buttered baking sheet and bake at 400 degrees for 30 minutes. Turn squash over and sprinkle with salt. Dot with butter.
Combine apple, finely grated, with the mincemeat and fill squash cavities; sprinkle with nuts. Bake 15 minutes longer. Sprinkle with nutmeg, freshly grated, before serving. Serves 6.

GROUSE

Rub each grouse with meat tenderizer and sprinkle with garlic salt. Sprinkle inside of birds with Italian seasoning. Melt ¼ cup butter in a dish (with cover) large enough to hold your birds. Brown on all sides and turn them breast side up.
Over each breast lay 2 strips of bacon. Add 2 cups chicken stock, ¼ cup white wine and 1 bay leaf to pot. Cover and roast in a 325 degree oven, basting often, for 2 hours or until tender.
Remove birds to a heated platter. Over high heat, reduce the liquid to ½ cup. Add 1 8-oz. jar currant jelly and stir until smooth. Spoon over grouse and serve.

BROWN SUGAR PIE

1 box brown sugar (1-lb.)
5 eggs
1 Tbs. butter, melted
3/4 cup warm water

1 tsp. vanilla
1 4-oz. can flaked coconut
2 unbaked pie shells (8-inch)

Beat eggs and sugar; add remaining ingredients and mix well. Pour into pie shells and bake at 350 degrees for 30 minutes or until firm. Makes 2 pies.

VENISON CURRY (CROCK POT)

3 lb. venison round steak,
   cut in 1½-inch cubes
½ cup flour
1 Tbs. curry powder
2 cloves garlic, minced
1 cup raisins
½ pint chutney (I use pear
   chutney)

1 cup diced onion
½ tsp. pepper
1 can beef broth (14 oz.)
2 unpeeled apples, cored and
   chopped
Rice

Mix flour and curry powder. Coat meat cubes with flour mixture. Place meat in crock pot. Add garlic, raisins, chutney,
onion and pepper. Pour in broth and stir to blend. Cover
and cook on LOW setting for 8-10 hours or until meat is
tender. Serve over hot rice. Serves 6 to 8.

--Susan O'Brien

*You may use venison, elk, or beef in this different chili
recipe...*

 ## EASY CHILI

1 Tbs. oil
1 large onion, coarsely
   chopped
2 cloves garlic, minced
1 lb. chili ground beef OR
1 lb. round steak cut in
   ½-inch cubes
2 Tbs. chili powder
1 Tbs. cocoa

1 tsp. salt
1 tsp. dried oregano, crushed
½ tsp. ground cumin
1 8-oz. can tomato sauce
   with mushrooms
1 cup water
2 cups cooked or canned dried
   pinto beans (optional)

In the hot oil, over low heat, brown the onion, garlic and
meat, stirring often. Add the seasonings, tomato sauce and
water; cook for 1 hour over low heat or until meat is tender.
(It will take longer for the cubed beef.) Add the beans and
cook another 30 minutes. Top with diced tomato, green
onions, and avocado when serving. Serves 4.

Life's A Bowl Of Berries

Early September is berry-picking time in the mountains. The area abounds with wild berries just waiting to be turned into delicious sauces, wines, jams and jellies. Wild currants grow in the Hahns Peak area, elderberries on Sand Mountain, and Buffalo berries...where else but Buffalo Pass. The more familiar chokecherries, serviceberries, wild raspberries, and gooseberries are found in abundance almost everywhere.

"It has been years and years since I have insulted a berry by cooking it. They are much too delicate and lovely to serve other than with sugar and cream," said Betty Neish who has a reputation for expertly cooking anything that grows. The recipe for strawberry mayonnaise is indeed "delicate and lovely."

STRAWBERRY MAYONNAISE

1 egg
1 Tbs. fresh lemon juice
1½ tsps. red wine vinegar
½ tsp. salt

3/4 cup light salad oil
1 Tbs. sugar
2 pints strawberries, sliced
  and lightly sweetened

In blender or food processor, blend egg, lemon juice, vinegar, and salt. On low to medium speed gradually add oil in a slow steady stream until mayonnaise is thick. Blend in sugar and a few berries for color. Chill well. Spoon chilled berries over watercress or salad greens and top with mayonnaise. Garnish with whole berries. You may substitute other fruits.. peaches or raspberries would be divine!

--Betty Neish

Of what, besides berries, do the words "delicate and lovely" remind you? Ladies luncheons, naturally. Steamboat is a bridge-playing town and most any week you will find ladies gathering for duplicate or just a friendly foursome. What a great time to prepare something extra special.

HAM AND CHICKEN ROLLS

2 cups cooked chicken, diced
4 green onions, chopped
1 tsp. dried tarragon
6 Tbs. sour cream
8 thin slices Swiss cheese

8 thin slices boiled ham
1½ cups thick cream sauce
¼ to ½ cup dry white wine
Dash of nutmeg
Salt and pepper to taste

Combine chicken, onions, tarragon and sour cream. Season
with salt to taste. Place the cheese slices on the ham
slices. Spoon onto the cheese side, some of the chicken
mixture and roll up; secure with a pick. Arrange, seam
side down, in a buttered baking dish. Flavor a thick cream
sauce with wine, a little more tarragon, nutmeg, salt and
pepper. Pour sauce over the ham rolls. Bake at 350 degrees
for 30 minutes. Serves 4 to 6.

ASPARAGUS AND PEAS

2 Tbs. butter
2 Tbs. flour
1 cup milk

1 can small green peas
1 can asparagus spears
1 cup sharp cheese, grated

Melt the butter in a saucepan; add flour and stir to blend.
Slowly add the milk and stir until thickened. Alternate layers of asparagus, peas and white sauce in a buttered casserole
dish. Top with grated cheese and bake 15 minutes at 350
degrees or until heated through. Serves 4 to 6.

--Terrell Parkerson

RASPBERRY ICE CREAM

2 pints fresh raspberries
   (or strawberries)
Juice of half lemon
½ cup sugar

½ cup water
3 egg yolks
2 cups cream

Mash berries and mix with lemon juice. Cook sugar and water
until syrup spins a thread (230 to 235 degrees). Beat egg
yolks until pale, gradually beating in the syrup until mixture is cool and thick. Stir in cream, raspberries and
juice. Taste for sweetness. Add powdered sugar if necessary.
Freeze in ice cream freezer to manufacturer's directions.

WATERGATE SALAD

1 large can chunk pineapple with juice
1 cup cottage cheese
1 cup Cool Whip

1 pkg. pistachio pudding and pie mix
1 cup pecans, chopped

Combine the ingredients and refrigerate until ready to serve. Serves 8.

--Susan Hoffner

COTTAGE CHEESE ROLLS

2 Tbs. yeast (2 pkgs.)
½ cup warm water
½ cup sugar
2 tsps. salt

½ tsp. baking soda
2 eggs
2 cups cottage cheese
4½ cups flour

Add yeast to warm water. Heat cottage cheese in a pan until warm; add sugar, salt, soda and eggs. Stir in yeast mixture. Add flour and mix well (no kneading necessary). Let rise in a warm place until double in bulk, at least 1 hour. Punch down. Divide dough into 24 balls. Place in a greased 13 x 9-inch pan. Bake at 350 degrees for 20 to 25 minutes or until nicely browned. Good with equal parts white and rye flour or white and whole wheat! Makes 24 rolls.

--Jan Vail

DALLAS DELIGHT

2 cups sugar
2 sticks butter, softened
6 eggs

1 12-oz. pkg vanilla wafers, crushed
1 cup pecans
1 7-oz. can flaked coconut

Grease a tube pan, line bottom with waxed paper, grease the paper. Mix ingredients in the order given and fill pan. Bake at 350 degrees for 1 hour and 15 minutes. Cake will keep a long time when refrigerated. A marvelous Christmas cake for those who do not care for candied fruits and citron.

POULET DE NORMANDIE

This is a wonderful company casserole because you do all the work the night before...great for bridge luncheons...ideal for leftover turkey or chicken around the holidays.

1 pkg. Peppridge Farm seasoned bread stuffing	1 stick melted margarine 1 cup water

Mix these together and put half of the mixture in a 12 x 5 casserole dish.

Combine the following:

2½ cups cooked, diced chicken	½ cup chopped celery
3/4 cup chopped onions, including green tops	½ cup mayonnaise ½ tsp. beau monde or seasoning salt
¼ cup chives, chopped	½ tsp. dry mustard

Put in casserole over bread mix. Top with remaining bread mixture.

Combine:

2 eggs, well beaten   1½ cups milk

Pour this mixture over the casserole. Cover with foil and refrigerate overnight or at least 6 hours. Take out of refrigerator about 1 hour before baking.

Spread with one can condensed cream of chicken or mushroom soup. Bake uncovered in 325 degree oven for 40 minutes. Serves 8.

--Shirley Finney

ARTICHOKE CASSEROLE

1 14-oz. can artichoke hearts, sliced in half	¼ cup water chestnuts, sliced 1 can mushroom soup
3 hard-cooked eggs, sliced	½ cup American cheese, grated
½ cup stuffed olives, sliced	½ cup buttered bread crumbs

Preheat oven to 350 degrees. Arrange artichokes in a casserole. Add a layer of eggs, olives, and chestnuts. Cover with soup. Top with grated cheese and bread crumbs. Bake until bubbly hot and crumbs are brown. Serves 4.

--Ann Coleman Smith

Whenever recipes are submitted for review by a cookbook committee, one always seems to stand clearly above the others. Usually this "super star" is widely acclaimed by good cooks and will be sponsored by several contributors. The following chocolate cake recipe was just such an overwhelming winner. Ironically, it was published in the original "Steamboat Simmers" and was given to me, among others, by my mother who is now 88 years old and still enjoys it!

GRANDMOTHER CAROTHERS' CHOCOLATE CAKE

½ cup margarine   ½ cup Crisco oil
3½ to 4 Tbs. cocoa   1 cup water

Combine in a saucepan and bring to a boil. In a large mixing bowl combine:

2 cups sifted flour   2 cups sugar

Add the butter mixture to the flour and sugar. Mix together:

2 eggs, well beaten   1 tsp. vanilla
1 tsp. soda   ½ cup buttermilk

Add the egg mixture to the other ingredients. Pour into a greased and floured 10 x 12 x 2-inch pan. Bake at 400 degrees for 25 minutes. After cake has been in oven for 20 minutes start making the icing.

Icing:

½ cup butter or margarine   1/3 cup milk
3½ Tbs. cocoa

Stirring constantly, bring to a rolling boil. Take from heat and add:

1 box powdered sugar   1 cup chopped pecans
1 tsp. vanilla

Pour over the cake while cake and icing are still hot. Cool and cut in squares to serve.

"Tis the dessert that graces all the feast,
for an ill end disparages the rest."
                                        William King

Rabbit Ears Pass

Rabbit Ears

"Out in Colorado deep within the mountain range
runs a stretch of highway that has taken many names.
Two thousand feet of winding grade waits for you in store
Seven miles until you reach the Yampa Valley floor."

Anthony Matthews - 1976
A Deep Powder Production

Rabbit Ears Pass was named for the rock formation north of
the pass summit which strongly resembles the ears of a
rabbit. The first road over the pass was built in 1913 and
originally was open only during the summer months. It was
not until 1928 that it was maintained for winter travel thus
attracting skiers who flocked to make the long run down the
back slopes of the pass to the base. WPA crews cut a trail
called Devil's Hangover providing a downhill course from the
west summit to a steep drop near The Timbers. Another
favorite course, Grannie's Delight, ran from near The Timbers south to Pleasant Valley.

Rabbit Ears Pass wears many dresses....spring green, the striking golds of fall, and the virgin white of winter. Even in this day of sophisticated snow removal equipment, driving over the pass in the dead of winter can be a harrowing experience. Whether skiing or driving, one should save this savory brew until reaching the Yampa Valley floor!

DEVIL'S HANGOVER

4 squares unsweetened
   chocolate, grated
4 cups light cream
2½ cups brandy

2 cups strong coffee
1¼ cups sugar
1 tsp. vanilla

Combine in a large saucepan and bring mixture to a simmer over low heat. Simmer, stirring, until chocolate melts. Fold in 1½ cups heavy cream, lightly whipped. Divide among 10 heat proof mugs to serve. Dust with nutmeg. Serves 10.

HIGH COUNTRY PUNCH:

Two cups cranberry juice cocktail, ½ cup orange flavor liqueur, 28-oz. bottle soda water and 1 (750ml) bottle white wine. Chill all ingredients and combine just before serving. Pretty served over an ice ring. Makes 9 cups.

HOT BUTTERED RUM MIX

¼ lb. butter (no substitute)
1 lb. dark brown sugar
¼ tsp. each, cinnamon,
   nutmeg, and cloves

Dark rum
Cinnamon sticks

Cream butter, sugar and spices thoroughly. Store in the refrigerator in a covered container. Place 1 heaping tablespoon of mix in a heated mug; add 1½ ounces dark rum and fill with boiling water. Stir with a cinnamon stick. Makes 1 drink.

--John Coleman

GRANNIES DELIGHT

1 cup sugar
1 cup nonfat dry milk powder
½ cup non-dairy creamer
½ cup unsweetened cocoa powder

3 Tbs. instant coffee crystals
1 tsp. grated allspice
Dash of salt
Cinnamon sticks

Combine all ingredients except cinnamon sticks. Store in an airtight container. For each serving: combine 3 tablespoons mix with 3/4 cup boiling water in a heat-proof mug; stir with a cinnamon stick to serve. Makes 2½ cups mix.

NOTE: This makes a lovely Christmas gift. Put mix in a decorative jar, tie with a bright ribbon and attach recipe and instructions for serving.

A drive to Meadows Campground near the west summit makes for a pleasant summer day. It was an early Indian campsite... perhaps they even hunted rabbits there. You need, however, go no further than the local supermarket on your hunt for this tasty meat so often overlooked by modern homemakers.

RABBIT EARS RABBIT

1 rabbit, cut in pieces
Vinegar
2 Tbs. salt
1 Tbs. pickling spices
1 Tbs. pepper

2 Tbs. flour
2 Tbs. butter
1 tsp. cinnamon
½ tsp. allspice
1 onion, chopped

Put rabbit pieces in a glass bowl or crock and cover with vinegar, salt, pickling spices, pepper and sliced onion. Marinate for 24 hours, covered. To cook, remove rabbit to a pan and cover with water. Gently boil until tender. Remove from pan and place in a baking dish. Brown butter and flour in a frying pan and add enough of the water rabbit was cooked in to make a thickened gravy. Add cinnamon, allspice, and chopped onion and cover rabbit with the gravy. Cover and simmer for 1 hour. Serves 4.

Or you might try rabbit stewed in a savory wine sauce.
Don't care for rabbit? Substitute chicken in either recipe!

RABBIT IN WINE SAUCE

¼ lb. bacon
½ lb. white boiling onions, peeled
1 2½ to 3-lb. rabbit, cut in pieces
½ cup sherry or white wine

2 to 3 cloves garlic, minced
2 Tbs. parsley, snipped
2 cups chicken stock
½ tsp. saffron (optional)
2 Tbs. soy sauce
¼ cup raisins

Fry bacon in skillet and drain on paper toweling; reserve.
Brown onions in bacon drippings for 5 minutes; reserve.
Brown rabbit pieces in bacon drippings over medium heat
about 10 minutes; add wine. Heat to boiling; add garlic and
parsley. Heat ½ cup of chicken stock to boiling and dissolve
saffron; add with remaining stock and soy sauce to the rabbit.
Cook, covered, until sauce is slightly thickened, about 20
minutes. Turn rabbit pieces to coat with sauce; add onions
and raisins. Simmer covered until rabbit is tender (10 to
20 minutes longer). Transfer to a serving platter; pour
sauce over rabbit. Crumble the reserved bacon over top of
rabbit. Serves 4.

SUMMER SQUASH CASSEROLE

6 cups yellow summer or
zucchini squash (or a combination or both) about 2 lb.
¼ cup chopped onion
1 can cream of chicken soup
1 cup dairy sour cream

1 cup shredded carrot
1 8-oz. pkg. herb seasoned stuffing mix
½ cup butter or margarine, melted

Clean and slice squash into ¼-inch slices. Cook in boiling
salted water with onion and carrots for 5 minutes. Drain
well. Combine soup and sour cream; stir in drained squash
mixture. Combine stuffing mix with butter; spread half on
bottom of baking dish. Cover stuffing mix with squash
and add remaining stuffing mix on top. Bake for 30 to 40
minutes at 350 degrees or until bubbly and hot. Serves 8.

--Shirley Zabel

FROZEN PEA AND BACON SALAD

1 pkg. frozen peas, thawed
2 green onions, chopped fine
5 slices lean bacon, fried
   crisp and crumbled

Salt and coarse ground pepper
½ cup sour cream

Rinse the thawed peas in cold water; drain well. Toss with
all the remaining ingredients and taste to correct seasonings. Use only enough sour cream to hold mixture together.
Chill. Serves 4.

--Anne Severson

*Near the pass are many lakes and streams filled with trout
just waiting to be caught. If you aren't handy with a fly
rod, try this recipe using thawed fish filets.*

BARBECUED TROUT OR SALMON

For each serving, cut 4 very thin slices through the backbone
of a very large trout. Allow about 1½ ounce per slice.
Marinate them for 2 hours in a good commercial barbecue
sauce. Remove from sauce and grill on each side about 2
minutes. Serve on a bed of rice pilaf and top with curry
sauce.

Curry Sauce:

1 tsp. butter
1 medium onion
1 medium apple
1 clove garlic
½ fresh tomato
2 tsp. mild curry powder

Salt
½ medium banana
1 quart fish stock
½ tsp. cornstarch
1 to 2 Tbs. dry white wine

Melt butter in a large skillet. Chop onion, apple, garlic,
and tomato and saute over low heat for 10 minutes. Add
curry, salt, banana and fish stock. Cook for 1 hour then
press through a strainer. Bring to a boil and thicken with
cornstarch dissolved in wine. This makes enough sauce for
12 portions of trout.

--Betty Neish

The Ute Indians of the Yampa Valley adorned their horses with colorful blankets, tied feathers in the mane and tail, and revered the animals which were such an important part of their everyday existence. They often traded their horses for the prized possessions of early settlers only to re-possess them in the dark of night. The Indian and his horse were never parted for long.

New settlers arrived breeding their horses with the Ute ponies; easterners brought thoroughbreds, and soon Colorado developed a reputation for excellence in horsebreeding. The horse has filled many needs in Colorado...transportation, ranching, farming, and now recreation. Guest ranches can be found in most mountain communities where "city dudes" are introduced to trail rides and scenic beauty inaccessible by car.

Rancher's Horses

There is nothing like a party of good friends heading for the trails at sundown for a campfire dinner. Guides are available and will even prepare your meal but if you decide to "do your own thing" you will find this marinade excellent for the steaks.

TERIYAKI FLANK STEAK

This is equally good with beef, elk, or venison steak.

1 large steak	1 Tbs. wine vinegar
¼ cup soy sauce	1 clove garlic, minced
2 Tbs. salad oil	½ tsp. ginger
2 Tbs. honey	

Combine and cover steak with sauce. Marinate for at least 2 hours, turning often. Broil to desired doneness, slice and serve. Serves 6.

--Judy Winograsky

NOODLE-APPLE CASSEROLE

2 cups boiled noodles	2 Tbs. sugar
4 apples, peeled and cut into eighths	Dash of salt
	Cinnamon to taste
4 Tbs. butter or margarine	

Melt 4 tablespoons butter in a baking dish and add half the cooked noodles. Top with all the apples and sprinkle with sugar, salt and cinnamon; top with remaining noodles. Bake, covered, at 350 degrees, for 10 minutes. Remove cover and bake an additional 30 minutes or until apples are soft and noodles are brown on top. Serves 6.

--Jane Romberg

QUICK SOUR CREAM BISCUITS: Combine 1 cup self-rising flour, ¼ tsp. soda and 3/4 cup sour cream. Turn dough out onto a lightly floured surface. Pat to ½-inch thickness and cut with a 2-inch biscuit cutter. Bake on a lightly greased cookie sheet at 450 degrees for 10 to 12 minutes. Makes 8 biscuits.

DRESSING FOR SUMMER FRUITS

2 cups plain yogurt
3 egg yolks
3 Tbs. honey

1 Tbs. curacao or brandy
1 Tbs. vanilla

In bottom of salad bowl beat together egg yolks, honey, brandy and vanilla. Fold in the yogurt and refrigerate until very cold. Serve over mixed fruits. This makes enough dressing for 6 to 8 cups fresh fruit.

--Lorna Brown

Barbara and Bob Day, owners of Storm Meadows Resort, were among the first major developers at the mountain. They make their home in Strawberry Park and their thoroughbred horses are known throughout the area. Barbara can be found riding early or late and likes to prepare things ahead of time so she can spend more time on the trail...

CHICKEN BROCCOLI CASSEROLE

4 large chicken breasts
¼ cup each minced onion
  and celery
2 10-oz. pkgs. frozen broccoli
1 can sliced mushrooms
4 Tbs. butter

4 Tbs. flour
2 cups milk
1 cup American cheese, grated
2 Tbs. sherry
Salt and pepper
1 cup Cheddar cheese, grated

Cover chicken with water and add the celery and onion. Bring to a boil, reduce heat and simmer 2 hours. Remove bones from chicken and cut the meat in large chunks. Reserve. Cook broccoli in salted water to package directions. Reserve. Melt butter in saucepan and stir in the flour to blend well. Gradually add the milk and cook until slightly thickened; add the American cheese. When cheese melts, add sherry, salt and pepper to taste.

Arrange layers of broccoli, mushrooms and chicken in buttered casserole; top with the cream sauce and sprinkle top with Cheddar cheese. Bake uncovered at 375 degrees for 30 minutes. Serves 6 to 8. This freezes well.

--Barbara Day

BUBBLE PIZZA BREAD

1 Tbs. butter or margarine
½ cup tomato sauce
2 tsp. instant minced onion
1 tsp. minced parsley
½ tsp. garlic salt

¼ tsp. oregano
1 Tbs. vegetable oil
1 can (10 biscuits)
  refrigerated biscuits
1/3 cup shredded Mozzarella
  cheese

Heat oven to 400 degrees. Melt butter in 8-inch round pan;
rotate to cover bottom of pan with butter or margarine. Combine tomato sauce, onion, parsley, garlic salt, oregano and
oil. Separate biscuit dough into 10 biscuits; cut each into
four pieces. Drop a few biscuit pieces at a time into tomato
mixture while tossing lightly with a fork. Place in buttered
pan and distribute evenly. Sprinkle with cheese. Bake at
400 degrees for 18 to 20 minutes or until golden brown. Cut
in wedges. Serve warm. Makes 6 servings.

For dessert Barbara makes a Pennsylvania Dutch treat...

SHOO FLY PIE

1 cup sifted flour
½ cup brown sugar
½ tsp. nutmeg
1 tsp. cinnamon
3 Tbs. butter

½ cup unsulfered molasses
½ cup hot water
½ tsp. soda
1 8-inch unbaked pie crust

Sift together flour, sugar, nutmeg and cinnamon; cut in the
butter as you would for a pie crust. Mix molasses, water and
soda. Pour into pie shell and sprinkle on the dry ingredients.
Dot the top with additional butter. Bake 10 minutes at 400
degrees; reduce heat to 350 and continue to bake for 35
minutes longer.

--Barbara Day

PUMPKIN BREAD: Combine 1 box pound cake mix, 2 eggs, 1 cup
pumpkin pie filling, 1/3 cup milk, ½ tsp. each
nutmeg and cinnamon. Mix to package directions and pour into
a greased loaf pan. Bake 1 hour and 15 minutes at 350
degrees.

--Nancy Bronennberg

Yampa, a little town in eastern Routt County, prospered in the late 1800's in the days of the large cattle ranches. In 1920, however, farmers discovered that lettuce and spinach would flourish in the area. It could be shipped by rail for $3.00 a crate and generated such profits that soon more than 2,000 acres were under cultivation. College students culti-vated small tracts, the profits paying for their education. Professional packers moved in from neighboring states but, strangest of all, the lettuce industry attracted a great number of Hindus to the area. They never gave up their native dress and the sight of white coats and turbans in fields of lettuce was indeed striking.

The lettuce and spinach industry enjoyed a boom for eight years before its decline and final demise in 1939 when a freeze and dry season caused farmers to abandon their fields. Gone are the white coats in lettuce fields...

The arrival of any ethnic group in a community produces new recipes. Research, however, failed to record any from the days of the Hindus in Yampa. Since curry is associated with their homeland, the following recipes are offered...reminis-cent of white coats and turbans.

CURRIED CHICKEN VICTOR

4 chicken breasts-skinned, boned and cut into 1-inch pieces
2 Tbs. butter
1 cup white wine
1 tsp. curry
20-25 chunks of pineapple

¼ cup heavy cream
Salt and pepper (white pepper is preferred but mandatory)
Pinch cayenne (optional)
1 tsp. parsley, chopped (optional)

Cook chicken in butter over medium heat until it turns white-about 4 minutes. It is important not to over-cook. Don't worry if the inside of the chicken is still a little pink. Remove chicken with slotted spoon to warm plate. Add the rest of the ingredients except parsley and reduce to half.

Now add the chicken and parsley and continue to reduce the liquid until the liquid has the consistency of a very light syrup. This should take another 4-5 minutes.

Serve with chopped almonds, fruit, long grain and wild rice, and snow pea pods. A California Chenin Blanc (well chilled) would go well with this meal. Serves 3 to 4.

--L. A. ("Vic") Vickrey

CHICKEN TANDOORI

8 to 10 assorted chicken
  pieces, preferably boned
2 large onions, chopped
2 cloves garlic, minced
2 small green peppers, seeded
2 tsps. salt
2 large tomatoes, peeled
  and chopped

1 Tbs. each ground curry
  powder, coriander, and cumin
1 tsp. tumeric
3/4 tsp. cinnamon
1 tsp. coarsely ground black
  pepper
½ cup butter, melted
2 cups chicken stock

Preheat oven to 375 degrees.
Place chicken pieces in a shallow buttered pan, skin side up. Sprinkle with onion, peppers, tomatoes, garlic and seasonings. Pour the melted butter over all. Carefully add the chicken stock and bake, basting often, for 1 hour. Serve with rice. Serves 4.

CUCUMBERS WITH YOGURT

To accompany any curried dish...

2 cups plain yogurt
2 cloves garlic, minced
Salt and freshly ground
  black pepper

Juice of 1 small lemon
1 cucumber, peeled, seeded,
  and finely chopped

Combine the ingredients and chill well before serving. Serves 6 to 8.

NOTE: The addition of 1 tsp. finely chopped fresh mint adds a refreshing taste change.

Lettuce is all too often taken lightly and used as a filler for salads. Here it stands with a filling all its own creating a very regal salad.

STUFFED LETTUCE

1 head iceberg lettuce
2 ozs. Roquefort or bleu
   cheese, softened
1 8-oz. pkg. cream cheese,
   softened

2 to 3 Tbs. cream
3 Tbs. finely chopped green
   onion
French dressing

Hollow out the center of lettuce leaving at least 1-inch shell. Beat cheeses and cream until smooth; add onion and mix thoroughly. Stuff lettuce with mixture. Chill until firm. To serve, cut into crosswise slices and serve with a good French dressing. Serves 4 to 6.

YAMPA SPINACH DIP

1 pkg. chopped frozen spinach
½ cup chopped parsley
2½ Tbs. chopped onion
1 tsp. salt

1 tsp. black pepper (this is
   the secret so do not
   decrease!)
Mayonnaise

Defrost spinach. Do not cook, but drain well. Combine with remaining ingredients using mayonnaise sparingly. Serve with a fresh vegetable tray or crackers. Makes 1 cup.

--*Cookbook Committee*

SPINACH MARY

2 pkgs. frozen chopped
   spinach
½ cup bread crumbs
1 pint sour cream

1 can onion rings
Salt and cayenne pepper
   to taste

Cook spinach to package directions and drain. Combine spinach, sour cream, onion rings (crumbled), seasonings, and half the bread crumbs. Put in buttered casserole and top with remaining bread crumbs. Bake at 350 degrees for 30 minutes or until bubbly and brown. Serves 8.

--*Jane Romberg*

MEXICAN LETTUCE SALAD

1 lb. ground beef
1 16-oz. can kidney beans,
  drained and washed
¼ tsp. salt
1 onion
4 tomatoes

1 head lettuce
4 ozs. grated Cheddar cheese
8 ozs. French dressing
1 avocado, peeled and sliced
1 8-oz. pkg. light corn chips

In a large skillet brown the ground beef; drain and add the kidney beans and salt. Simmer for 10 minutes. Combine the onion, tomatoes, lettuce, cheese and dressing. While meat mixture is still hot and just as you are ready to serve, toss with the tomato mixture. Fold in the avocado slices and corn chips last. Serves 6 to 8.

--Ruth McGuyrt

TORTILLA TID-BIT:

Spread flour tortillas with softened cream cheese; sprinkle with chives and parsley flakes. Roll the tortillas and cut into thirds. Pass a mild chili salsa for dipping if desired. Serve as an accompaniment to the Mexican Lettuce Salad or with cocktails.

--Ruth McGuyrt

COLORADO EGG ROLLS

1 pkg. egg roll skins
2 cups seafood, chopped
  (crab, shrimp, scallops)
2 large cans whole green
  chilies
2 cups grated Jack cheese

Salt and cayenne pepper to
  taste
Egg
Oil for frying
Salsa and sour cream

Combine seafood and Jack cheese and season with salt and cayenne. Place a green chili in center of egg roll skin and slit down the middle. Fill with seafood mixture. Brush edges of skin with beaten egg and fold in side corners over the chili. Roll tightly and brush the entire surface of egg roll with beaten egg to seal. Fry in deep oil until lightly browned. Serve with a sauce made by combining salsa and sour cream to your taste. Serves 6.

--Sheri Stephens

LETTUCE FIELD SALAD

½ cup slivered almonds
2 Tbs. sugar
1 head iceberg lettuce
1 cup chopped celery

3 or 4 whole green onions, chopped
1 11-oz. can Mandarin oranges, drained

Combine sugar and almonds in a skillet over medium high heat. Shake the skillet to keep from burning but do not stir. When almonds are coated thoroughly turn out onto waxed paper. Cool and break apart.

Dressing:

½ tsp. salt
Pepper to taste
¼ cup oil

1 Tbs. chopped parsley
2 Tbs. each sugar and vinegar
Dash of Tabasco

Combine the dressing ingredients. Break lettuce into bite size pieces and combine with celery, onions and oranges. When ready to serve, toss with dressing and add the almonds. Serves 6 to 8.

--Tina Richie

The elegant orange salad goes well with the equally elegant...

LAMB WITH SOUR CREAM

2 Tbs. cooking oil
3 lbs. boneless lamb shoulder, cubed
½ tsp. salt
Dash of paprika
2 small onions, diced
2 cups tomato juice

1 Tbs. minced parsley
1 sprig fresh sweet marjoram
OR
1 pinch, each, dried marjoram and summer savory
Fresh mint
1 cup sour cream

Heat oil in a fireproof casserole with a lid. Add lamb, from which all fat has been removed and into which salt and paprika have been rubbed. Brown meat lightly, add onion, then stir in tomato juice, parsley and herbs. Cover and simmer on top of stove for 2 hours, or bake in oven at 300 degrees for 2 hours. Add a little hot water if the juice boils too low. Just before serving, stir in sour cream, mixing well. Garnish the platter with sprigs of fresh mint.

The reddish colored soil of the local area, particularly along
the creek banks, gave the parks their names, and legend gives
us this interesting anecdote...

In the early 1900's the first range wars between cattlemen
and sheepherders took place in the parks located in the Hahn's
Peak area. The Routt National Forest had issued permits for
sheep from Wyoming to graze along the Park Range and eleven
bands were located in Whiskey and Red Parks. Oscar Walker,
an ex-saloon keeper from Brooklyn's "red light district," saw
a chance to make some easy money. He carted a wagon load of
whiskey and three girls from Cheetel's house of ill repute
into the area on pay day. Enchanted by their visitors, the
herders left the sheep unattended to mix it up with the girls.
Meanwhile, eleven bands of sheep did a little mixing on their
own. Seems they had quite a time getting them separated and
much delay and confusion in the trail drive was caused by
the female distraction, human and animal!

The park supervisor became so incensed over the situation that
he tied the leader of the Brooklyn girls to a tree and refused
to release her until she promised that she and her companions
would leave the park. It didn't take her long to agree to do
so, but the supervisor wanted her to remember well this occasion. He cut off her hair, tied it with a piece of ribbon,
and hung it in the Whiskey Park Ranger Station where it remained for many years.

*A new haircut tied with a ribbon? You look and feel great!
Send the kids to grandma'a house for the night, set a table
for two before a roaring fire, pop a bottle of champagne, and
serve your husband lamb in fond remembrance of the sheepherders...*

BARBECUED LAMB CHOPS

Soy-Lemon Basting Sauce:

1 Tbs. brown sugar	2 Tbs. water
1 tsp. cornstarch	2 Tbs. sliced green onion
2 Tbs. lemon juice	1 Tbs. butter or margarine
2 Tbs. soy sauce	1 clove garlic, minced

In saucepan, blend brown sugar and cornstarch. Stir in lemon juice, soy sauce, and water. Add onion, butter and garlic. Cook, stirring, until thickened and bubbly. Grill chops over medium coals. Baste during last 15 minutes of cooking. Makes about 1/3 cup of sauce.

--Joyce Taylor

If your spouse isn't fond of lamb, poor soul, substitute this unusual dish of pork chops...

HUNGARIAN VICTOR'S PORK CHOPS

2 loin pork chops 1-inch thick	¼ tsp. white pepper
1 small onion, thinly sliced	Dash garlic powder
¼ tsp. caraway seed	1¼ cups white or rose' wine
½ tsp. salt	(dry is preferred)
¼ tsp. paprika	½ cup sour cream
¼ tsp. dried dill weed	Cooking oil or butter

Trim excess fat from chops. Brown chops over hot fire. Remove chops and discard liquid fat. IMMEDIATELY deglaze pan by pouring wine into pan and scraping with a wooden spoon. Add all of the rest of the ingredients except the sour cream to the pan. Then add the chops. Cover and cook over a low fire until there is a moderate firmness to the touch...about 30 minutes. Transfer chops to a warm platter. Stir sour cream into pan and reduce until the consistency of very light syrup. Strain sauce over chops. Serves 2.

--L. A. "Vic" Vickrey

AND, you can always please everyone with spareribs...takes time to prepare them right but the end result is worth the effort!

LAZY TOM'S SWEET AND SOUR RIBS

2 to 3 cloves garlic, minced
1/3 cup honey
¼ cup soy sauce
½ cup catsup
1 14-oz. can beef broth

4 lbs. lean pork spareribs or beef short ribs
4 tsps. each cornstarch and water

In a small saucepan combine all ingredients except cornstarch and water. Bring to a boil then set aside. Cut ribs apart and arrange closely, fitting in a large baking dish. Marinate several hours or overnight in the refrigerator. Bake, covered, at 350 degrees for 1½ hours; remove cover and continue baking, basting often, another hour or until tender. Remove ribs from pan. Skim the fat from the drippings and discard. Combine cornstarch and water and stir into the liquid over low heat just until thickened. Use as a sauce for ribs. Serves 6.

--*Maggie Subr*

BAKED TOMATOES

2 small ripe tomatoes
Italian salad dressing
1 green onion, minced

1 small jar marinated artichokes
Basil, cracker crumbs, lemon pepper, Parmesan Cheese

Early in the day peel the tomatoes and cut a slice from the top. Pour a generous tablespoon of the salad dressing over each tomato and sprinkle with the green onion. Cover and refrigerate. One hour before cooking, remove from refrigerator; slice two artichoke hearts for each tomato and place on top. Combine the remaining ingredients and sprinkle over tomatoes; top with a dab of butter. Bake at 350 degrees for 20 minutes. Serves 2.

The baked tomatoes would go well with either of the following to round out your menu...

BAKED CREAMED CORN

2 Tbs. cornstarch
2 eggs
¼ cup sugar

1 can evaporated milk
1 16-oz. can cream style corn
2 Tbs. melted butter

Combine cornstarch, eggs, and sugar; mix well. Add milk and corn; mix again. Pour into a buttered casserole dish (about 2 inches deep) and pour melted butter on top. Bake at 325 degrees for 1 hour or until firm. Serves 4 to 6.

--Maggie Subr

CHEESE POTATOES

3 lbs. potatoes
1 16-oz. carton sour cream
1 large jar Cheese Whiz

1 can cream of mushroom soup
½ cup green onions, chopped

Peel and cut potatoes in large dice. Cook until barely tender. Drain and combine with the remaining ingredients. Pour into a buttered baking dish and bake at 300 degrees for 2 hours. Serves 12.

--Carolyn Williams

TOFFEE NUT PEAR CAKE

2 fresh Bartlett pears, cored
  and cut into eighths
2 cups flour
½ tsp. salt
1 tsp. cinnamon
¼ tsp. nutmeg
2 cups brown sugar

½ cup butter
1 tsp. baking soda
1 cup sour cream
1 egg
½ cup chopped nuts
Sweetened whipping cream
  (optional)

Sift flour with salt, cinnamon and nutmeg. Mix in brown sugar. Cut in butter with pastry blender until crumbly. Generously grease a 9-inch square baking dish. Spoon in half the flour-butter mixture and press evenly over bottom of pan. Arrange pears over crust. Stir baking soda into sour cream and mix into remaining flour-butter mixture along with the

129

egg. Pour batter over pear slices and spread evenly.
Sprinkle with chopped nuts. Bake at 350 degrees for 40 to
50 minutes. Serve warm with sweetened whipped cream if
desired.

--Diane Franklin

FRUIT PUNCH BARS

2¼ cups flour
1½ tsps. soda
½ tsp. salt
2 eggs
1½ cups sugar

1 16-oz. can fruit cocktail
  (do not drain)
1 tsp. vanilla
1-1/3 cups coconut
½ cup chopped nuts

Sift flour with soda and salt. Grease and flour bottom of a
15 x 10 x 1-inch jelly roll pan. Beat eggs and sugar in a
large bowl at high speed until light and fluffy; add fruit
cocktail, flour and vanilla and beat at medium speed until
blended. Spread into prepared pan, sprinkle with coconut
and nuts. Bake at 350 degrees for 20 to 25 minutes. While
hot, drizzle with glaze of icing. Serves 8.

--June Kinney

SWEET AND SOUR MEATBALLS

1 lb. lean ground beef
1 egg
1 tsp. salt
1 Tbs. minced onion
1 Tbs. cornstarch
2 Tbs. oil

1 cup water
½ cup pineapple juice
1/3 cup pineapple tid-bits
½ green pepper, cut in strips
8 Marashino cherries
1 pkg. sweet and sour mix

Combine beef, egg, salt, pepper, onion and cornstarch. Shape
into marble sized meatballs. Heat oil in skillet and brown
the meatballs. Remove from pan and clean skillet. Drain
pineapple, reserving ½ cup of juice. Combine water, juice
and sauce mix in skillet and cook, stirring constantly, until
thickened. Add meatballs, pineapple, peppers and cherries.
Cook 5 minutes or until heated through. Serve over rice.
Serves 4 to 6.

--Betty Christoff

Nipple Peak

Do you ever feel like letting the men in your family know who really is boss? Seems one Maggie Baggs, common-law wife of George Baggs, did this regularly. She cussed out everyone in sight, "took advantage" of the cowhands on their Double Eleven Ranch and horsewhipped cowboy Jack Farrell in public. Because of its distinctive shape Jack had referred to a promontory in the Hahns Peak area as 'Maggie's Nipple" and had suffered the consequences.

But ladies beware, lest your fate be the same as Maggie's. She became enamoured of a red-haired cowboy, left the ranch she could "boss" around, and when her settlement money was gone so was the red-head. She ended up in Texas managing a "rooming house." When you're in the Hahn's Peak area take a look at Nipple Peak and think of Maggie. Then go home and fix your "Boss" a special dinner...

CHILLED CUCUMBER SOUP

1 large cucumber, peeled and sliced
1 tsp. dill weed
½ cup snipped parsley
¼ cup lemon juice
2 Tbs. vinegar
¼ cup snipped chives
1/3 cup grated onion

½ tsp. dehydrated onion
¼ tsp. white pepper
1 Tbs. powdered chicken bouillon
1 cup water
2 Tbs. sugar
1 quart buttermilk

Put all ingredients except buttermilk in blender and blend until fine consistency. Add to buttermilk, mix well and chill for several hours before serving. Makes 1 quart.

--Maggie Subr

PARMESAN BREAD SLICES: Cut French or sourdough bread into ½-inch slices. Brush both sides with a hearty bottled Italian dressing. Sprinkle topside with finely chopped walnuts and grated Parmesan cheese. Heat on a baking sheet for 5 to 10 minutes or until lightly browned. Serve hot.

STUFFED STEAK

1 large thin round steak	¼ cup green olives, sliced
Salt	Fresh bread crumbs
1 onion, sliced into rings	4 Tbs. melted butter
1 small jar pimientos, sliced	1 cup Burgundy
1 4-oz. can mushroom pieces	

Pound the steak until very thin. Salt meat and cover with onion rings, pimiento, mushrooms, green olives and bread crumbs. Sprinkle with melted butter until moist. Roll up into a long roll and put in a buttered loaf pan. Cover with the wine and cook at 350 degrees for 1 hour or until nicely browned. Serve sliced with either brown gravy or hollandaise sauce. Serves 4.

--Ruth Valdeck

STRAWBERRY AND SPINACH SALAD

10 ozs. fresh spinach, coarsely torn
1 lb. fresh strawberries

Lemon Dressing:

¼ cup sugar	1 egg yolk
3 Tbs. fresh lemon juice	6 Tbs. vegetable oil

Clean spinach very well and place in a salad bowl. Arrange berries atop spinach and chill. Add lemon juice to sugar and whisk until sugar is nearly dissolved. Add yolk and continue whisking until all sugar is dissolved. Add oil 1 Tbs. at a time, whisking constantly until dressing is thick and creamy. Cover and refrigerate. Pour dressing over salad and toss gently to serve. Serves 6.

--Diane Franklin

LOBSTER IN BUTTER: 1½ cups cooked lobster cut in large pieces. Heat ½ cup butter in saute pan and add lobster and 1 tablespoon lemon juice and cook until hot. Add ½ cup slivered almonds, 1 cup cream mixed with 2 egg yolks and 2 tablespoons minced parsley. Heat until sauce thickens and serve over rice. Serves 4.

Poverty Flats

The name does little to conjure up thoughts of gambling, dancing girls, liquor, and riotous living which characterized the town in 1880. The village of Poverty Flats later became the town of Hahns Peak. It was the campsite for miners searching for gold and silver at the Poverty Bar Placer Mine, one of the largest in the area. Both the village and the mine are listed in the Colorado Inventory of Historic Sites.

Poverty flat would be an apt description of most grocery budgets just before pay day! Maybe there's not enough left in the account to feed dancing girls, but if you're a gambler you might spend your last cent on a new economy recipe to excite your family...

POOR MAN'S RACLETTE

Fromage a raclette is a semi-soft cheese traditionally melted before a roaring fire, scraped onto a hot plate, and served with boiled potatoes, marinated onions, and tiny sweet pickles. If you can't find (or can't afford) authentic raclette which is usually sold in cheese specialty shops, substitute Monterrey Jack, Muenster or Caraway Swiss.

Serve as appetizer or main course.

1 lb. Caraway Swiss cheese
2 potatoes, peeled and boiled

Marinated onions
Sweet pickles

Cut the cheese into about ½-inch thick slices. Arrange them overlapping in shallow baking dishes for individual servings. Broil about 4 inches from heat for 5 minutes or until bubbly and brown. Dip chunks of potato, onions and pickles in cheese and ENJOY! Best served with a dry white wine. Serves 2 to 4.

Marinated onions:

3 cups mild red or white
   onions, thinly sliced
½ cup tarragon vinegar

1 tsp. sugar
½ tsp. salt

Separate onions into rings and mix with remaining ingredients.

                                         --Ruth McGuyrt

SALMON SALAD PIE

1 pkg. frozen broccoli spears	3 hard cooked eggs, diced
1 unbaked 9-inch pie shell	½ tsp. dill weed
1 7-3/4 oz. can salmon, drained and flaked	1 cup shredded Swiss cheese
1/3 cup diced celery	1 cup mayonnaise
¼ cup sliced green onions	Dash of pepper

Cook broccoli; drain and arrange in pie shell. Fold salmon, celery, green onions, egg, dill, pepper and cheese into mayonnaise. Spoon over broccoli. Bake at 375 degrees for 30 minutes. Good served cold or warm. Serves 6.

--Ethel Taylor
Denver, Colorado

BAKED HAM CASSEROLE

¼ cup butter or margarine	¼ medium-size green pepper, cut in strips
¼ cup honey	
1 Tbs. soy sauce	1 16-oz. can apricots, drained and cut in slivers
2 tsps. Dijon mustard	
2 cups cooked rice	2 cups diced cooked ham

Preheat oven to 350 degrees. Place butter in a 1½-quart casserole dish and set in oven to melt. Remove from oven; add honey, soy sauce and mustard; mix well. Add remaining ingredients and toss to cover with sauce. Bake 45 minutes to 1 hour. Serves 6.

ITALIAN ZUCCHINI CASSEROLE

1 lb. ground beef	1 to 2 cups Cheddar cheese, grated
Salt and pepper	
3 small zucchini, sliced	2 cups cottage cheese
1 medium onion, chopped	2 eggs, beaten
3 Tbs. butter	Parmesan cheese & paprika
1 small can green chilies	

Season meat with salt and pepper and brown slightly. Cook zucchini and onion until softened and mash with 3 tablespoons butter. Add green chilies. In a buttered baking dish, arrange a layer of ground beef, top with zucchini mixture

and sprinkle with grated cheese. Combine cottage cheese and
eggs and spread on top; sprinkle with Parmesan and paprika.
Bake at 350 degrees for 30 minutes. Let stand a few minutes
before serving. Serves 6.

--Lillian Hagan

PASTA CARBONARA

½ lb. bacon, chopped
½ medium onion, chopped
1 large clove garlic, minced
2 to 3 sprigs parsley,
  chopped

½ cup olive oil
1 lb. linguine or home made
  pasta, cooked and drained
2 eggs beaten

Brown bacon lightly; add onion, garlic and olive oil; saute
lightly. In bowl or shallow baking dish, beat the eggs; add
hot pasta and toss. Add the bacon sauce and keep tossing;
the heat from the pasta will cook the eggs. Sprinkle with
grated cheese and parsley and serve immediately. Pass additional cheese when served. Serves 4 to 6.

--Anne Severson

PUMPKIN MUFFINS

In a large bowl sift:

2 cups all purpose flour
2 cups cake flour
1¼ cups sugar
2 tsp. baking powder

1 tsp. salt
1¼ tsp. cinnamon
1¼ tsp. freshly ground nutmeg

In another bowl combine:

1½ cups milk
1¼ cups pumpkin

½ cup PLUS 2 Tbs. butter,
  melted and cooled
2 eggs (lightly beaten)

Add to flour mixture. Stir until just combined. Fold in 1
cup raisins. Fill muffin pans 2/3 full. Sprinkle top with
sugar. Bake at 400 degrees for 20 minutes or until done -
about 20 minutes.

--Marilynn Finn
Carlisle, Pa.

Dead Mexican Park

Dead Mexican Park, located in the Hahns Peak area, is listed in the Colorado Inventory of Historic Sites. It's a strange name for such a peaceful park. Two sheepherders, Quintana and Velasquez, didn't find it so peaceful in 1915, however. They were employed by the Carbon County Sheep Company and were murdered in their sleep by one Joe Belardi. Legend has it that Joe was quite a gambler and had lost his own and the herders' wages in a poker game. Unable to admit his folly to his companions, he killed them, set fire to the camp, and disappeared. The two Mexican sheepherders are buried in the park; its name is a memorial to them.

Mexican food has gained immensely in popularity over the years. "Tex-Mex" is a combination of the authentic cuisine of our Mexican neighbors and Texas imagination...often running rampant. Easy to prepare, the following menu would make a delightful informal buffet with a south-of-the-border flavor.

MARGARITAS

3 ozs. tequila	2 cups ice
Juice of 2 limes	Salt
1 oz. Triple Sec	

Blend all ingredients except salt in an electric blender. Wet the rim of a glass; invert on a heavily salted towel. Strain the mixture into the salt rimmed glass and serve. Serves 2.

JOSEFINAS

4 hard rolls	½ cup mayonnaise
1 3-oz. can chopped green chilies	4 ozs. Jack cheese, grated
½ cup butter	3 Tbs. Parmesan cheese, grated
2 large cloves garlic, minced	Cayenne pepper

Slice rolls into ½-inch slices; toast on 1 side. Combine chilies, butter and garlic. Spread on untoasted side of each roll slice. Combine mayonnaise and Jack cheese; spread on butter mixture and dust with Parmesan cheese and a sprinkling of cayenne. Broil until cheese is brown and puffy. Makes about 20 appetizers.

TEX-MEX DIP

3 medium avocados
2 Tbs. lemon juice
½ tsp. salt
¼ tsp. pepper
1 cup sour cream
½ cup mayonnaise
1 pkg. taco seasoning mix
2 10½-oz. cans plain or
  jalapeno flavored bean dip

1 cup green onion, chopped
3 medium tomatoes, coarsely
  chopped
2 3½-oz. cans chopped ripe
  olives
8 ozs. Cheddar cheese, grated
Large tortilla chips

Pit, peel and mash the avocados in bowl with lemon juice, salt and pepper. Combine sour cream, mayonnaise, and taco mix in bowl. To assemble, spread bean dip on a large shallow serving platter; top with seasoned avocado mixture. Layer with sour cream taco seasoning mixture. Sprinkle with chopped onions, tomatoes, and olives; top with cheese. Serve chilled or at room temperature with chips for dipping. Serves 6 to 8 generously with drinks.

--Carol Mitchell

SKILLET ENCHILADAS

1 lb. ground beef
½ cup chopped onion
1 10½-oz. can cream of
  mushroom soup
1 10-oz. can enchilada sauce
1/3 cup milk

2 Tbs. seeded, chopped green
  chilies (canned)
8 tortillas
Cooking oil
2½ cups sharp cheese, grated
½ cup ripe olives, pitted

In a 10-inch skillet brown the ground beef and onion; drain off excess fat. Stir in soup, enchilada sauce, milk, and chilies. Reduce heat to low; cover and cook 20 minutes, stirring occasionally. In a small skillet dip the tortillas in hot cooking oil just until limp; drain. Place ¼ cup of cheese on each tortilla; sprinkle with olives. Roll up each tortilla and place in the sauce. Cover and cook until heated through (about 5 minutes). Sprinkle with remaining cheese (½ cup); cover and cook only until cheese melts, about 1 minute. Serves 4.

--*Marci Weber*

MEXICAN CASSEROLE

1 lb. ground beef	¼ tsp. garlic powder
½ green pepper, chopped	Salt and pepper to taste
1 small onion, chopped	1 16-oz. can tamales
1 16-oz. can tomato sauce	1 to 2 cups corn chips,
½ Tbs. chili powder	crushed
¼ tsp. cumin powder	2 cups grated Cheddar cheese

Brown meat over medium heat; add green pepper and onion and saute until onions are transparent. Drain off fat. Add tomato sauce and seasonings. Simmer over low heat for 15 minutes. Unwrap tamales and cut into 1-inch pieces. Pour meat mixture over the tamales in a greased baking dish. Top with grated cheese and sprinkle with the crushed corn chips. Bake at 350 degrees for 30 minutes. Serves 4 to 6.

--*Deb Link*

Mexican food is spicy and filling. A tossed salad with a tart dressing would certainly be sufficient for a family dinner. Something more elaborate should grace a party buffet table.

AVOCADO SALAD RING

2 Tbs. unflavored gelatin	1 small onion
½ cup hot water	3 ripe avocados, peeled and
1½ cups orange juice	diced
1 Tbs. sugar	Few drops of Tabasco
1 tsp. salt	Orange and grapefruit
2 Tbs. pickle relish	sections, watercress and
1/3 cup lemon juice	mayonnaise

Dissolve gelatin in water. Add remaining ingredients and blend until smooth in electric blender or food processor. Pour into an oiled ring mold and chill until set. When ready

to serve, turn out onto a bed of watercress. Fill center
with fruit sections and serve with mayonnaise thinned with a
little heavy cream. Serves 8.

PASTA FRUIT SALAD

1 cup sugar
2 Tbs. flour
Dash of salt
2 eggs, beaten
1-2/3 cups pineapple juice
1¼ cups Grandini or
  Cini di peppe
Salted water

1 16-oz. can crushed
  pineapple, drained
1 16-oz. can pineapple
  chunks, drained and cut in
  half
2 cans Mandarin oranges,
  drained
9 ozs. non-dairy whipped
  topping

Cook sugar, flour, salt, eggs and pineapple juice over medium
heat until thickened. Reserve and cool completely. Cook the
pasta in salted water 6 to 8 minutes; drain and cool. Combine
the cooled dressing and pasta. Add pineapple and Mandarin
oranges and fold in the whipped topping. Let cool in refrigerator until serving time. Serves 12.   --Betty Christoff

POOR MAN'S SPICE CAKE

1 box raisins
2 cups sugar
1 tsp. cinnamon
1 tsp. cloves
2 tsps. nutmeg

3 heaping Tbs. shortening
2 cups + 3 Tbs. cold water
3 cups flour
1 tsp. baking soda
4 Tbs. hot water

Combine raisins, sugar, cinnamon, cloves, nutmeg, shortening and cold water in a saucepan. Boil for 5 minutes;
remove from heat and let cool. Add the flour. Mix the soda
with hot water (it will foam) and add to batter. Stir well
and pour into a greased and floured 9 x 13-inch cake pan.
Bake at 350 degrees for 45 minutes or until cake tests done.
It is good plain, served with whipped cream, or you can
frost it with confectioners' sugar mixed with orange juice
to spreading consistency.   --Deb Link

Steamboat Lake Park

Two picturesque lakes are located in Steamboat Lake Park, an easy 27-mile drive from Steamboat Springs. Pearl Lake is open only for wakeless boating and Steamboat Lake is popular with water skiers. Billy Kidd, former Olympic skier of renown, takes to the water in July to host his annual Billy Kidd Hobie Cat Regatta on Steamboat Lake. Hundreds of racers compete in this colorful event with red sails against a backdrop of mountains.

When winter blows its icy breath across the lakes, the basin becomes a wonderland for cross country skiing, snowmobiling, and ice fishing. It was designated a State Park Area in 1970.

Whether you catch your fish from the cold mountain streams of summer or in a frozen lake in winter, fresh from the water is best. Not all anglers are successful, particularly the once-a-year fisherman. So best you have some trout in the freezer to accommodate the unlucky sportsman.

SHRIMP AND CRAB STUFFED TROUT

2 Tbs. butter or margarine	¼ to ½ cup fine bread crumbs
1 clove garlic	1 Tbs. minced parsley
1 small onion, chopped	1 Tbs. minced chives
½ medium green pepper, minced	¼ tsp. salt
¼ lb. cooked crab, flaked	1/8 tsp. pepper
¼ lb. tiny shrimp	4 10-inch trout

Melt butter. Add garlic and onions and saute until onion is transparent. Add green pepper, crab, shrimp, bread crumbs, parsley, chives, salt and pepper. Mix well, adding more crumbs if needed to hold mixture together. Brush trout with additional melted butter and pile stuffing in cavities. Place in a greased close-fitting pan and bake covered at 350 degrees for 15 minutes. Uncover and continue to bake another 30 minutes or until trout tests done. If you have leftover stuffing, bake it in the pan with the trout. Serves 4.

--Kitty Ellison

SPINACH RICE CASSEROLE

2 cups cooked rice
1 10-oz. pkg. frozen chopped
  spinach
1 large onion, chopped

½ cup butter, cut in chunks
1 16-oz. box Velveeta cheese,
  cut in chunks*

Cook spinach and drain very well. Combine spinach with the
remaining ingredients in a 2-quart casserole. Cover and bake
at 350 degrees for 15 minutes; remove cover and bake an additional 15 to 30 minutes or until hot and bubbly. Serves 8.

*Can use Cheddar.

--Elaine Stroncek

Toss a salad of everything green and serve with Bleu Cheese
Dressing...

JEAN'S BLEU CHEESE DRESSING

½ quart mayonnaise
1 4-oz. cube Roquefort or
  bleu cheese
¼ tsp. garlic powder

¼ tsp. pepper
¼ tsp. Worcestershire Sauce
Dash of Tabasco Sauce
1 cup buttermilk

Combine all the ingredients in a blender (or mix by hand).
Bleu cheese should remain "lumpy" so do not over-blend.
Cream can be added to make the dressing thinner if desired.

--Jean Neas

GRANDMA'S CARROT CAKE

3/4 cup safflower oil
1 cup sugar
2 cups flour
1 tsp. baking powder
1 tsp. cinnamon

¼ tsp. salt
1 cup raw carrots, grated
2 eggs, beaten
½ cup chopped nuts
½ tsp. vanilla

Mix all ingredients as listed and pour into a well greased
loaf or tube pan. Bake at 350 degrees for 1 hour. Cool
and glaze as desired.

--Kristin and Billy Kidd

141

Many people are turning away from the use of meats in their diets. Some will use chicken or fish sparingly, but many refuse anything but vegetables. If your guest is a vegetarian, it need not present a problem. In fact, it might help your health AND your budget if you plan to serve at least one vegetarian meal each week!

GARDEN VEGETABLE DELIGHT

1 16-oz. can tomato sauce
¼ cup water
2 tsps. Worcestershire sauce
1 tsp. salt
¼ tsp. oregano
2 medium cloves garlic, crushed

Combine all the ingredients, mix well, and set aside.

1 eggplant, peeled and cut into ¼-inch slices
2 medium zucchini, cut into ¼-inch slices
1 cup uncooked spaghetti, broken
3 medium celery stalks, chopped
1 green pepper, chopped
8 ozs. mozzarella slices

In a greased shallow 9 x 13-inch casserole, arrange half of the eggplant slices in a single layer. Layer over half of the zucchini, spaghetti, celery, and green pepper. Cut mozzarella slices into 18 to 20 pieces and layer half over the vegetables. Spoon on half the tomato sauce mixture. Repeat layers. Bake, covered, at 350 degrees for 1 hour and 15 minutes. Can be made the day before baking and refrigerated. Serves 6 to 8.

--Regina Hollberg
Englewood, Colorado

CHEESE BALL

2 8-oz. pkgs. cream cheese
1 8-oz can crushed pineapple, well drained
¼ cup chopped bell pepper
2 Tbs. chopped onions
1 Tbs. seasoned salt
1 cup chopped pecans
1 cup chopped pecans to roll balls in

Mix all ingredients together except 1 cup chopped pecans. Make into 2 balls. Roll balls in 1 cup chopped pecans. Chill.

--Mae Bryant

BROCCOLI QUICHE WITH WHEAT GERM CRUST

2/3 cup unbleached flour
1/3 cup each, quick cooking
  oats, raw wheat germ
6 Tbs. cold butter or
  margarine
3 Tbs. cold water
1 lb. broccoli

Salt, pepper
½ tsp. dill weed
3 eggs
1/3 cup each, milk, mayonnaise,
  unflavored yogurt
2 cups grated sharp cheese

Mix together flour, oats and wheat germ. Using a pastry
blender, cut in butter to make coarse crumbs. Add water and
stir with a fork to make a pastry ball. Roll out and place
in a greased 9-inch pie plate; trim excess and crimp edges.

Chop broccoli into ½-inch pieces (should have about 4 cups)
and steam above water for 4 to 5 minutes, or until tender
crisp. Put in bottom of the pie shell. Sprinkle with salt,
pepper and dill weed. Beat together eggs, milk, mayonnaise
and yogurt. Stir in cheese. Spread over broccoli and bake
at 350 degrees for 35 minutes or until set. Cool slightly
before serving. Serves 6.

FETTUCCINE WITH ZUCCHINI AND MUSHROOMS

2 Tbs. salt
1 Tbs. vegetable or peanut oil
12 ozs. fettuccine
8 ozs. fresh mushrooms, sliced
¼ cup butter or margarine
1¼ lbs. small zucchini, cut
  into 2½-inch strips
1 cup heavy cream

½ cup butter or margarine,
  cut up
3/4 cup freshly grated
  Parmesan cheese
¼ cup snipped parsley
¼ cup pitted ripe olives,
  sliced
Salt and pepper

Bring a large amount of water to boiling; add salt and oil.
Cook pasta for 7 minutes. Drain well. Meanwhile, in a large
skillet cook mushrooms in the first ¼ cup butter over medium-
high heat for 2 minutes. Add zucchini, cream, and the remaining butter. Bring to boil; simmer, covered, about 3 minutes.
Add cooked pasta to mushroom mixture in skillet. Add Parmesan,
parsley and ripe olives, tossing till all is mixed. Season
to taste with salt and pepper. Serve at once sprinkled with
additional Parmesan cheese. Serves 10 to 12.

CREAMED EGGS AND MUSHROOMS

½ lb. medium-sized fresh
  mushrooms or 1 can (6 to
  8 ozs.) whole mushrooms
6 Tbs. butter or margarine,
  divided
3 Tbs. flour
3/4 tsp. salt

1½ cups half and half
2 tsps. Worcestershire sauce
5 hard-cooked eggs
2 Tbs. pimiento strips
1 pkg. (10-oz.) frozen patty
  shells, baked

Rinse mushrooms and pat dry or drain canned mushrooms; cut
in halves. In a small skillet heat 2 tablespoons of the
butter until hot. Add mushrooms; saute until mushrooms are
golden, about 5 minutes; set aside. In a medium saucepan
heat remaining 4 tablespoons butter. Stir in flour and salt
until smooth. Blend in cream; cook and stir constantly,
until thickened. Stir in Worcestershire sauce; simmer for
1 minute. Cut eggs into wedges. Stir eggs, pimiento, and
reserved mushrooms into sauce. Heat until hot. Spoon into
patty shells. Garnish with parsley sprigs, if desired.

CAULIFLOWER NUT LOAF

Good as a main course or side dish.

2 lbs. cauliflower, cut up
5/8 cup vegetable stock
½ lb. grated cheese
2 ozs. grated walnuts

1 Tbs. whole wheat flour
4 ozs. cheese crackers,
  crumbled
¼ tsp. nutmeg

Steam cauliflower in vegetable stock until quite soft. Blend
cauliflower with remaining stock and add all ingredients but
reserve half the cheese. Turn mixture into an oiled casserole and top with remaining cheese and additional walnuts.
Bake at 350 degrees for about 35 minutes.

--Kristin and Billy Kidd

SHRIMP-RICE CASSEROLE: Combine 2 cups each cooked shrimp,
                       cooked rice, and heavy cream. Add
6 tablespoons catsup, and 1 tablespoon each Worcestershire
and Tabasco sauce. Bake, uncovered, at 350 degrees for 25
minutes. Serves 6.

Up! Up! And Away

There's more than one way to get "up in the air" in Steamboat Springs. The timid can take the usual jet flight leaving several times daily or the adventuresome can pop a bottle of champagne and drift above the mountain peaks in a colorful balloon. If neither appeals to you, consider the gondola which rises 2,000 feet above the valley floor commanding an unparalleled view of several mountain ranges. Plan to spend several hours at the top strolling the trails so loved by wintertime skiers.

Not content to leave the balloons with an "Around The World In 80 Days" image, the west has added a cowboy touch to the art of racing this ungainly mode of travel. Would you believe a Balloon Rodeo? This combines balloon racing and lassoing of wooden horses from the air. With more than 30 balloons aloft over snow-capped mountains, the event is a kaleidescope of color.

If you are "up in the air" about what to prepare for dinner after partaking of any or all the aforementioned thrills, try one of these easy chicken recipes when you get your feet back on the ground...

RICE AND CHICKEN IN FOIL

For each serving, wrap the following in heavy duty foil:

2 pieces of frying chicken   1 tsp. dry onion soup mix
1 serving cooked rice   Pinch Chinese five spice
                                       seasonining

Cover each with undiluted cream of mushroom soup. Bake 1 hour at 375 degrees.

--Kathie Smith

SWEET AND SOUR CHICKEN

1 cup apricot preserves
1 bottle Russian dressing
1 pkg. dry onion soup mix
6 to 8 chicken breasts

Combine preserves, dressing and soup mix. Pour over chicken and bake uncovered in a buttered dish at 325 degrees for 1 hour. Baste occasionally. Serves 4.

--Jean Consalus

ARGENTINIAN CHICKEN SALAD

6 small boneless chicken
  breasts
2 small green peppers
1 can large pitted black
  olives
4 tomatoes, peeled and seeded
1 large red onion
2 small cans chopped green
  chilies

1 large jar pimiento strips
6 cloves fresh garlic, chopped
3 Tbs. cilantro, chopped
Salt and cayenne
½ Tbs. cumin
1½ cups olive oil
½ cup red wine vinegar
3 avocados
Tortilla chips

Cook chicken, remove skin and cut in bite size pieces. Cut green pepper in large pieces and cut olives in half. Cut red onion in 1-inch strips and tomatoes in large pieces. Combine the chicken and vegetables with pimientos, green chilies, garlic, salt, cayenne, cilantro, and cumin. Add olive oil and vinegar. Marinate in refrigerator for one hour. Serve over half an avocado with tortilla chips on the side. Serves 6 to 8.

--Sheri Stephens
CJ's Restaurant

CREAMY CHICKEN PATE: Combine 1 5-oz. can chunky chicken, 8 ozs. cream cheese with chives, ¼ cup crushed pineapple in heavy syrup (drained), ¼ cup toasted pecans or almonds, 3 Tbs. chopped pimiento and dried dill weed to taste. Serve with crackers.

This could be cooking while you are flying high in the wild blue yonder...

CHICKEN THIGHS VICTOR (CROCK POT)

8 chicken thighs, skin removed	¼ tsp. ground cardamom
1 can chicken broth	1½ Tbs. cornstarch
1 can mushroom soup	24 black pitted olives, halved
1 tsp. salt	2 tomatoes, skin removed,
¼ tsp. white pepper	quartered
¼ tsp. poultry seasoning	½ lb. mushrooms, quartered

Place first 7 ingredients (through cardamom) in crock pot and cook on LOW for 3 hours.
Turn crock pot to HIGH and add final 5 ingredients. To prevent lumping, mix the cornstarch with a little water before adding to crock pot.
Cook for an additional 30 minutes on HIGH. Serve with long grain rice and a big salad. Serves 4.

A well chilled Chablis or Chardonnay goes well with this meal.
--L.A. "Vic" Vickrey

Just as quick and easy to prepare are the following seafood flights of fancy.

BAKED FISH FILETS

Frozen filets, thawed OR	1/3 cup lemon juice
1 trout per person	1 cup butter or margarine
1 small green pepper, chopped	1½ cups brown sugar
1 small onion, chopped	

Saute onion and green pepper in butter; add lemon juice and brown sugar. Pour over fish. Bake at 350 degrees for 45 minutes or until fish flakes easily. This can also be done outside over hot coals. Place fish in heavy duty foil, pour dressing over and seal into packages. Cook until fish tests done.
--Mike Rafter

HALIBUT ALYESKA

The kitchen crew on the "Alaska Explorer" gave me this gorgeous, yummy recipe!

3 lbs. halibut steaks
1½ cups sour cream
½ cup mayonnaise
2 Tbs. chopped onion

3 Tbs. lemon juice
Salt and pepper
1 cup Cheddar cheese, grated

Put fish steaks in a buttered glass baking dish. Combine the remaining ingredients and cover fish. Bake at 375 degrees for 25 minutes.

NOTE: We have tried canned Bumble Bee sockeye salmon with this recipe and it is just as good.

--Laura Ann Bennett

SHRIMP CASSEROLE

1 lb. shrimp, cooked
Salt and pepper
½ lb. mushrooms, sliced
3 Tbs. butter
1 Tbs. flour

1 cup sour cream
5 Tbs. butter
1 tsp. soy sauce
¼ cup Parmesan cheese
1 tsp. Hungarian paprika

Put the cooked shrimp in a buttered baking dish (one just large enough to hold them in one layer). Sprinkle with salt and pepper to taste. Saute mushrooms in butter until browned; stir in the flour and gently add the sour cream and remaining butter, soy sauce and additional salt and pepper if desired. Pour over the shrimp, sprinkle with cheese and paprika. Bake at 400 degrees for 10 minutes. Serves 4.

CHUTNEY SHRIMP: Saute ½ cup chopped onion in ¼ cup butter until golden. Stir in 2½ tsps. curry powder and ½ cup bottled chutney; mix well. Add 3 cups cooked small shrimp (or large chopped) and heat but do not boil. Spoon over rice or pastry shells and sprinkle with finely chopped hard-cooked egg and parsley. Serves 4.

Snow began to fall on an early March day in 1929 and during the next 24 hours 30 inches had accumulated over an existing base of 27 inches...it was the heaviest single snowfall in recorded Steamboat history. The early settlers made good use of their homemade skis during similar days. They were first used in Routt County to carry mail in 1880 when George Wren and Elmer Brooks, Sr. skied to a cabin on Morrison Creek to meet the mail carrier who skied in from Rock Creek. Often in the 1920's the Salt Lake and Pacific train was snowbound, cutting Steamboat off from the outside world. Hearty settlers donned their skis and relieved their cabin fever by skiing into Denver, a two-week journey.

If a heavy snowstorm in the mountains or a rainstorm in the city keep you inside, cooking soup is a marvelous way to relieve your cabin fever. Or if you feel creative, prepare several things to freeze for later use...

STEAK SOUP

1 lb. round steak, cut in small cubes
½ lb. butter or margarine
1 cup flour
½ gallon water
1 stalk celery
½ #303 can tomatoes

Fresh ground pepper
1 large carrot, diced
1 medium onion, diced
1 10-oz. pkg. frozen mixed vegetables
4 Tbs. beef flavor base

Make a roux; melt butter, stir in flour and gradually add 2 cups of water. Stir until smooth. Add remaining ingredients except cubed steak; set aside. In another pan, saute steak in 2 Tbs. butter until browned; drain off fat. Add meat to first mixture and simmer, stirring occasionally for 1½ hours or until vegetables are tender. If soup needs thickening, add more roux. May be frozen for later use.

--*Carol Mitchell*

149

TURKEY SOUP EXTRAORDINAIRE

1 cup diced cooked turkey
3 cups turkey or chicken broth
¼ cup butter
2 Tbs. chopped onion
1 tsp. curry powder
1 cup diced potatoes
½ cup diced carrots
½ cup diced celery

Salt and pepper
½ pkg. frozen French cut
   string beans
1 tsp. fresh oregano (or
   ½ tsp. dry)
1 Tbs. minced parsley
1-2/3 cups light cream
2 Tbs. flour

Melt butter in a large pot and cook onion until transparent.
Stir in curry powder and cook for 1 minute. Add broth,
potatoes, carrots, celery and seasonings. Bring to a boil,
reduce heat and cook for 15 minutes. Stir in green beans,
turkey, oregano, and parsley. Continue cooking for 15
minutes. Combine half and half and flour and add to soup,
stirring until thickened. Check seasonings. Serves 4.

--Regina Hollberg

CABBAGE AND CRANBERRY SOUP

2 cups cranberries, coarsely
   chopped
3 onions, chopped
3 cups cabbage, finely
   shredded
3 Tbs. brown sugar

1 Tbs. salt
Pepper to taste
3 10½-oz. cans chicken broth
1 16-oz. can diced beets
Sour cream

In a large pot, toss together cranberries, onions and
cabbage; add sugar, salt and pepper. Add broth plus enough
water to equal 6 cups liquid. Cook about 20 minutes or until
vegetables are very tender. Add beets and their liquid; heat
through. Serve garnished with sour cream. Serves 6.

Cold wintry days and soups bubbling on the stove go hand in hand. Make a double recipe...one for dinner and one to freeze for later.

CHEESY OYSTER SOUP

6 green onions, chopped, tops too!
¼ cup green pepper, chopped
¼ cup red pepper, chopped
2 Tbs. butter
2 cups milk
1 8-oz. pkg. cream cheese and chives

1 pint oysters, drained
2 cups chicken broth
½ tsp. salt
Pepper to taste
Dash of Worcestershire sauce

Saute onion, green and red peppers in butter in a large pot. Add milk and cream cheese; cook over low heat, stirring until cheese melts and mixture is smooth. Add the remaining ingredients and simmer until edges of oysters begin to curl, about 7 minutes. Garnish with parsley if desired. Makes 7 cups.

SHRIMP GUMBO

1 16-oz. bag frozen cut okra
3 large onions, sliced
3 cloves garlic, minced
½ lb. hot sausage, diced or sliced
1 bay leaf
Salt and pepper to taste

½ tsp. crushed red pepper (or more to taste)
1 16-oz. can stewed tomatoes
1 8-oz. can tomato sauce
2 cups water
2 lbs. frozen peeled and deveined shrimp

Combine all ingredients except shrimp. Simmer 30 minutes over low heat. Add shrimp and simmer an additional 15 minutes. Serve over hot rice if desired. Serves 6.

A Time To Remember

A town you call home remains always a part of your life.
First you remember the people and your house, and then little
events start spinning in your mind like a kaleidoscope...

I remember my first ski lesson. Billy Kidd had helped me buy
my boots and skis, so I thought some of his magic would keep
me on my feet. No such luck. I spent most of my time in a
prone position staring up at my all to handsome instructor.

I recall Dorothy Wither...very lovingly. She introduced me
to Mrs. John Love, the governor's wife, as I stood in the
Dorothy Shop fitting room...in my underwear!

And the time I gave a party honoring my visiting parents when
someone called (I can't remember who) and asked if they might
bring Frank Gifford and Don Meredith. I spent the evening
swooning -- the party was a big success.

Golfing...Ladies' Days and trips to Rifle and Craig for tour-
naments. I never scored very well except for one day.
Through a trick of fate I had to play my best friend, Ruth
McGuyrt, for the monthly club championship. I had never beat
her before (or since) but I WON! How sweet it was.

I recall vividly the crisp winter nights when the stars were
close enough to touch and the snow crunched under my boots.
And the quivering, shimmering aspen leaves -- green springs
and golden falls.

Bridge parties...one after the other. Helping to form the
duplicate club which is still in existence. All those lovely
snowy days spent at a table with good friends and a quarter
on the corner.

And finally, STEAMBOAT SIMMERS, my first cookbook. The thrill
of writing it after the many interviews and finally seeing it
in print. Little did I realize that it would lead to my own
television shows, newspaper column, and the even bigger thrill
of writing a second edition.

All those memories bring a smile, but if I had to set apart a single day it would be one on the ski hill with Ruth McGuyrt. It was January. Christmas tourists had departed and a champagne powder snow had fallen during the night. The day dawned bright and clear and very early Ruth called suggesting that we be the first on the hill. As we rode the lift it was like ascending into fairyland. The snow clung to the trees like ornaments and the cloudless sky was too blue to be true.

We skied down the trail to Bear Claw and, without a moment's hesitation, Ruth went sailing off the top. Trembling, I followed. Imagine my surprise when I couldn't see my skis -- nor could I see Ruth's legs below her knees. We were skiing in unpacked powder snow. And then I fell...which was like a marshmallow explosion! Everything went "pouff." The soft, fluffy snow flew up around me and I laughed like a child. Falling was actually fun -- an incident which I repeated several times. When I finally caught up with Ruth we looked up to see our ski trails in the snow. Mine were marked by marshmallow explosions. At the top of the run a Thikol was starting its packing trip down the hill, erasing the imprints of our beautiful day. As we giggled our way down Giggle Gulch I thought to myself, "This is a day I shall never forget" ---and I haven't. It was indeed a time to remember.

 A MARSHMALLOW EXPLOSION

40 large marshmallows, cut
   three times
1 cup white wine
1 cup pecans

2 cups whipped cream
1 box ladyfingers
Whole cherries

Pour wine over the cut marshmallows and let stand, covered, in the refrigerator overnight. Add the pecans and fold in the whipped cream just before serving. Line ladyfingers around the edge of a large compote and fill with the marshmallow mixture. Garnish with whole cherries. Serves 8.

Note: You may use small jelly rolls filled with jam and cut
      in thin slices instead of the ladyfingers; kiwi fruit
      as a garnish is beautiful!

SNOW TOPPED CHICKEN CASSEROLE

3 cups cooked rice
1 16-oz. can cut asparagus
  spears and tips
2 cups cooked chicken or
  turkey, cubed
1¼ tsps. salt

¼ cup slivered almonds
1/8 tsp. black pepper
1 small onion, minced
1 cup heavy cream, whipped
1½ cups Cheddar cheese, grated

Combine rice, asparagus, turkey, almonds, pepper and 1 teaspoon of the salt. Spoon into a buttered 10-inch, deep-dish
pie plate (or casserole dish). Whip the cream to stiff
peaks; add the remaining salt and grated cheese; spread over
the chicken mixture. Bake at 350 degrees for 30 minutes.
Serves 6.

WHITE FLUFF

2 16-oz. cans pineapple
  chunks, drained
1 16-oz. jar Queen Anne
  cherries, pitted and
  drained

1 cup miniature marshmallows
½ cup toasted slivered
  almonds or pecans

Dressing:

2 egg whites, beaten stiff
¼ cup sugar
3/4 tsp. salt

2 Tbs. vinegar
2 Tbs. lemon juice
1 cup whipping cream, whipped

Whip all the dressing ingredients except whipping cream together in the top of a double boiler. Cook over simmering
water until thickened; about 5 to 7 minutes, stirring constantly. Chill the mixture thoroughly and add the whipping
cream, whipped to stiff peaks. Add the drained fruit,
marshmallows and nuts; stir to blend. Serves 6 to 8.

SNOW PIE

Light and airy, just like Steamboat's champagne powder!

1 envelope plain gelatin	1 tsp. vanilla
3 egg whites	Pinch of salt
2/3 cup sugar	1 cup hot water

Dissolve gelatin in 3 Tbs. cold water for 5 minutes in a large mixing bowl. Pour hot water on gelatin and stir until clear. Let cool. Add unbeaten egg whites, vanilla, sugar and salt. Beat at high speed with electric mixer for 15 minutes or until thick and creamy. Pour into a 9-inch pie plate. Refrigerate until firm. Serve with Lemon Sauce.

Lemon Sauce:

3 egg yolks	2 Tbs. lemon juice
1/3 cup sugar	1 Tbs. grated lemon peel
1/3 cup melted butter	1/3 cup heavy cream, whipped

Beat egg yolks well and add sugar; mix well and add melted butter, lemon juice and grated peel. Fold in whipped cream.

--Alison Lambart

"THE DAINTIEST LAST TO MAKE THE END MORE SWEET."

-- Shakespeare

Index

Peanut Brittle................... 38
Peanut Butter Crisps............. 11
Pecan Crunch..................... 73
Raspberry Ice Cream............. 108
Rhubarb Dream Bars............... 31
Rice Krispie Dessert............. 64
Seven Layer Bars................. 52
Triple Peanut Cookies............ 38

EGGS-CHEESE (MEATLESS)

Bacon and Egg Strata............. 40
Broccoli Quiche................. 143
Brunch Eggs...................... 17
Brunch Eggs Elegante............. 24
Cauliflower Nut Loaf............ 144
Cheese Ravioli................... 43
Creamed Eggs and Mushrooms...... 144
Crescent Zucchini Pie............ 22
Eggs Pasta - Pesto Sauce......... 42
Fettuccini with Zucchini........ 143
Garden Vegetable Delight........ 142
Mushroom Casserole............... 15
Noodle-Apple Casserole.......... 118
Pesto Potatoes................... 44
Raclette........................ 133

FISH-SEAFOOD

Baked Fish...................... 147
Barbecued Trout................. 116
Chutney Shrimp.................. 148
Colorado Egg Rolls.............. 124
Crabmeat Souffle................. 23
Halibut Alyeska................. 148
Lobster in Butter............... 132
Peachy Shrimp.................... 86
Scalloped Corn and Oysters....... 81
Shrimp Casserole................ 148
Shrimp-Rice Casserole........... 144
Stuffed Trout................... 140
Trout in Champagne............... 27
Tuna Treasure.................... 77

MEATS

Beef:
Beef Stew with Wine............. 33
Bologna Salad................... 76
Cheddar Burgers................. 87
Deviled Hamburgers.............. 89

Dill Pickle Rolls............... 35
Easy Chili..................... 106
Impossible Reuben Pie........... 70
Italian Zucchini Casserole...... 134
Meatballs-Red Sauce............. 44
Mexican Casserole.............. 138
Mexican Lettuce Salad.......... 124
Skillet Enchiladas............. 137
Smoky Brisket................... 90
Spaghetti Pie.................. 100
Stove Top Meatballs............. 53
Stuffed Steak.................. 132
Sweet and Sour Meatballs....... 130
Teriyaki Flank................. 118

Game:
Easy Chili..................... 106
Elk In A Pumpkin............... 104
Fruited Venison Stew............ 62
Grouse......................... 105
Rabbit in Wine................. 115
Rabbit Stew.................... 114
Venison Curry.................. 106
Venison Kabobs................. 103

Lamb:
Barbecued Lamb Chops........... 126
Lamb in Cabbage................. 27
Lamb with Sour Cream........... 125

Pork:
Baked Ham Casserole............ 134
Barbecued Sausages.............. 75
Chop Suey...................... 100
Cold Ham Mousse.................. 9
Glazed Sausages................. 17
Ham and Chicken Rolls.......... 108
Ham and Strawberries............ 80
Hungarian Chops................ 126
Italian Sausage Quiche.......... 95
Jambon Veronique................ 57
Onion Pie (Bacon)............... 12
Pasta Carbonara................ 135
Sausage and Cheese Skillet...... 96
Sausage and Rice Casserole...... 95
Stuffed Sweet Potatoes.......... 14
Sweet and Sour Ribs............ 128

PIES-MOUSSES

Almond Topped Cheese Cake......... 59

Blueberry Topped Cheese Pie...... 19
Brown Sugar..................... 105
Cherry Delight.................. 97
Fudge Sundae.................... 86
John's Rhubarb.................. 25
Kahlua Mousse................... 68
Marshmallow Explosion........... 153
Molded French Cream............. 58
Oatmeal Date.................... 65
Pot De Creme.................... 28
Raspberry or Strawberry Sorbet... 69
Satin Pie....................... 34
Shoo-Fly........................ 120
Snow Ice Cream..................
Snow Pie........................ 155
Strawberries Romanoff........... 80
Strawberry 7-Up................. 80
Strawberry Mousse............... 79
Summer Pear-Cheese Pastry....... 50
Sweet Potato.................... 13
Swiss Chocolate................. 21
Tom's Pecan..................... 36

POULTRY

Argentinian Chicken Salad........ 146
Chicken and Ham Rolls........... 108
Chicken Almondzini.............. 81
Chicken Broccoli................ 119
Chicken Cacciatore.............. 21
Chicken Tandoori................ 122
Chicken Tetrazzini.............. 91
Chicken Thighs Victor........... 147
Chicken in Foil................. 145
Citrus Chicken.................. 72
Company Chicken................. 69
Curried Chicken................. 121
Poulet de Normandie............. 110
Roasted Chicken................. 10
Saturday Night Chicken.......... 85
Smoky Galliano Chicken.......... 84
Snow Topped Chicken............. 154
Sweet and Sour.................. 146
Turkey-Cheese Casserole......... 92

RELISHES-SAUCES

Apple Cider Syrup............... 40
Blue Cheese Dressing............ 141
Carrot and Apricot Relish....... 14

Dressing for Summer Fruit........ 113
Italian Red..................... 44
Pear Pickles.................... 93
Pesto Sauce..................... 42
Rhubarb Preserves............... 38
Sauce for Ham................... 73
Strawberry Butter............... 80
Strawberry Mayonnaise........... 107
Summer Fruit Dressing........... 119
Sweet Pepper Chili Sauce........ 47
Watermelon Pickles.............. 93

SALADS

Apricot Orange.................. 85
Argentinian Chicken............. 146
Asparagus....................... 26
Avocado Ring.................... 138
Avocado-Citrus.................. 79
Bologna......................... 76
Carrot.......................... 13
Cherry.......................... 94
Cherry-Coke..................... 24
Cucumbers with Yogurt........... 122
Frozen Fruit.................... 33
Frozen Slaw..................... 88
Lettuce Field Salad............. 125
Melon with Prosciutto........... 45
Mexican Lettuce................. 124
Molded Pineapple................ 89
Pasta Fruit..................... 139
Pea and Bacon................... 116
Sauerkraut...................... 75
Spinach......................... 101
Strawberry Spinach.............. 132
Stuffed Lettuce................. 123
Summer Fruit.................... 119
Watergate....................... 109
White Fluff..................... 154

SANDWICHES

Celebration Cucumber............ 29
Chipped Ham..................... 46
Orange on Marmalade Bread....... 30
Peachy Croissant................ 48
Pizza Sandwich.................. 46
Roquefort Topped Chicken........ 49
Sandwich Surprise............... 48
Watercress Rounds............... 30

Historical Index

ROUTT MEMORIAL HOSPITAL AUXILIARY
P.O. BOX 1899
STEAMBOAT SPRINGS, CO 80477

Please send me _____ copies of MORE STEAMBOAT SIMMERS at
$6.00 per copy. I am enclosing $1.25 to cover postage and
handling.

NAME _____

ADDRESS _____

CITY _____ STATE _____ ZIP _____

ROUTT MEMORIAL HOSPITAL AUXILIARY
P.O. BOX 1899
STEAMBOAT SPRINGS, CO 80477

Please send me _____ copies of MORE STEAMBOAT SIMMERS at
$6.00 per copy. I am enclosing $1.25 to cover postage and
handling.

NAME _____

ADDRESS _____

CITY _____ STATE _____ ZIP _____

ROUTT MEMORIAL HOSPITAL AUXILIARY
P.O. BOX 1899
STEAMBOAT SPRINGS, CO 80477

Please send me _____ copies of MORE STEAMBOAT SIMMERS at
$6.00 per copy. I am enclosing $1.25 to cover postage and
handling.

NAME _____

ADDRESS _____

CITY _____ STATE _____ ZIP _____